The Art of Mediumship

Psychic Investigation, Clairvoyance, and Channeling

Elaine Kuzmeskus

Schiffer Publishing Ltd

4880 Lower Valley Road, Atglen, Pennsylvania 19310

Other Schiffer Books by the Author:

Connecticut Ghosts   0-7643-2361-X $9.95
Séance 101   978-0-7643-2717-9 $19.95

Schiffer Books are available at special discounts for bulk purchases for sales promotions or premiums. Special editions, including personalized covers, corporate imprints, and excerpts can be created in large quantities for special needs. For more information contact the publisher:

Published by Schiffer Publishing Ltd.
4880 Lower Valley Road
Atglen, PA 19310
Phone: (610) 593-1777; Fax: (610) 593-2002
E-mail: Info@schifferbooks.com

For the largest selection of fine reference books on this and related subjects, please visit our website at **www.schifferbooks.com**
We are always looking for people to write books on new and related subjects. If you have an idea for a book, please contact us at
proposals@schifferbooks.com

This book may be purchased from the publisher.
Include $5.00 for shipping.
Please try your bookstore first.
You may write for a free catalog.

In Europe, Schiffer books are distributed by
Bushwood Books
6 Marksbury Ave.
Kew Gardens
Surrey TW9 4JF England
Phone: 44 (0) 20 8392 8585; Fax: 44 (0) 20 8392 9876
E-mail: info@bushwoodbooks.co.uk
Website: www.bushwoodbooks.co.uk

Copyright © 2012 by Elaine Kusmeskus

Library of Congress Control Number: 2012932903

Designed by Stephanie Daugherty
Type set in Papyrus/NewBskvll BT

ISBN: 978-0-7643-4016-1
Printed in the United States of America

Contents

Elaine Kuzmeskus, Director of the New England School of Metaphysics, is a nationally known Spiritualist medium. She first made contact with her Hindu guide in her crib. Other guides soon followed. By twenty-two, she joined a development circle led by Rev. Gladys Custance and Rev. Kenneth Custance to unfold her gift of mediumship and was certified as a Spiritualist medium in 1972. Since then she has served many Spiritualist churches and camps, including Lily Dale Assembly in New York. In 1997, Elaine Kuzmeskus conducted the Official Houdini Séance. Spirit has even played a role in her writing.

The ancient Egyptians, Tibetans, Greeks, and modern Spiritualism provided answers to the riddle of death through the art of mediumship. Mediums such as the Fox Sisters and Reverend Andrew Jackson Davis started the Spiritualist movement which swept the country in the late 1800s and reached its peak in the 1920s.

Premiere mediums such as Clifford Bias, Arthur Ford, Mable Riffle, Mamie Schultz Brown, Richard Zenor, Ann Gehman, and Brian Hurst were trained in the Spiritualist tradition. Today's mediums, Sylvia Browne, James Van Praagh, John Edwards, and Suzanne Northrop are stage mediums who demonstrate their abilities to packed audiences all over the country. Whether for church or stage, they took time to develop their unique gifts. Learn more about their development and the guides who assist them.

Science Examines the Afterlife

Scientists from Professor William James to Dr. Gary Schwartz have studied mediums with scientific precision. What information does science provide about the afterlife?

Natural Law

Just as the earth plane has a code of conduct, so the spirit world has its laws. What are these and how do they affect development?

Varieties of Mental and Physical Mediumship

Clairsentience, clairaudience, and clairvoyance are examples of mental mediumship. Physical mediumship includes table tipping, electronic voice phenomena (EVP), and psychic photography. However, there are also less-known aspects of both mental and physical mediumship.

Dream Visitations

Spirit is just a thought a way. The most natural way to reach deceased loved ones is through meditation and dreams. Learn how to use meditation and dreams to tune into spirit.

Mediation Portal to the Other Side

Meditation is the most common way to connect with spirit. Learn how meditate and contact the other side.

Spirit Guides

Guides are an essential part of mediumship. Not only do they assist in your development, they act as protectors, chemists, and inspiration.

Table Tipping, Levitation, Spoon-Bending, and Apports

Table tipping was a craze during Victorian times, much like today's interest in spoon bending. Some mediums could even levitate and produce apports!

Channeling

As the students progress with mediumship, their level of trance will naturally deepen. However, many student wish to obtain a state of "dead trance." What conditions are needed for the development of deep trance mediumship? Trance mediums Elwood Babbitt and Jane Roberts, J. Z. Knight, have added much to our understanding of death and dying.

What Really Happens in a Séance

Séances can range from private sittings to formal séances by invitation only to public demonstrations to mediumship. What is the best way to gain credentials and credibility with the public? How should a medium deal with a skeptic? Learn what really happens in a séance.

A Professional Medium

As a professional medium, the author has worked in a variety of settings and visited many spiritual sites. What is it like to be a professional medium? What are her most recent adventures with spirit?

Dedication

This book is dedicated to my students at the New England School of Metaphysics, Suffield, Connecticut. As always, I have so much to share with you. Please keep in mind as you pursue your course of study that mediumship combined with meditation, spiritual guidance, and compassion is a noble profession. May *The Art of Mediumship* enhance your skills as mediums and seekers of Truth. Remember, too, the words of The Prophet:

> *"Say not, 'I have found the truth,'*
> *but rather, 'I have found a truth.'"*

> ~Kahil Gibran

Acknowledgments

I would like to take this opportunity to thank the many people who have made this book possible. First, my husband, Ronald Kuzmeskus, who accompanied me on trips throughout the United States, England, and Brazil. His photography skills, clairvoyance, and sense of humor were indispensable. Next, I would like to thank Susan Roberts for her careful editing and help in crafting the book. It is always a pleasure to work with a friend. Finally, I would like to thank Dinah Roseberry of Schiffer Publishing for her assistance and enthusiastic support. She is blessed with both intuitive insight and literary skills.

Introduction

Adventures With Spirit

As a medium, I am frequently asked, "How do you really know you are in contact with the spirit world?" The first thing that comes to mind is personal experience. Ever since I was in my crib, I have seen spirits. The first one that I remember was a bare-chested Hindu guide with a white muslin turban. As the years have passed, other guides have made their presence known – an Egyptian, an ancient Chinese physician, Dr. Andrew Lang, an English researcher, Dr. Johnson, an African-American physician, and noted medium, Rev. Arthur Ford. Occasionally, writers such as Jack Kerouac and Rod Serling have come in to assist when I am writing a metaphysical book.

Psychic experiences are another way I know when I am in contact with the other side. My intuition has always been accurate. I remember peering through a microscope at a drop of hand lotion my third grade teacher, Mrs. McGinty, had us observe. As I looked at the pattern of pink bubbles, I suddenly "knew" that was my birthday present, even though my birthday – March 25 – was the day before and I did not expect any more gifts. I also knew I wasn't getting a microscope or hand lotion. Unable to fathom why I had this persistent thought, I put it out of my mind. However, when I returned home from school, my grandmother handed me a box embossed with pink bubbles. "This is your birthday present, Elaine. Your Aunt Polly and Uncle John couldn't make it to your party and wanted you to have this." While I cannot recall the bracelet inside, I will never forget the box the gift came in!

Even though I had many psychic experiences as a child, it wasn't until I was a junior in college that I began to seriously explore the psychic realm. The catalyst was the then recent best seller, *The Sleeping Prophet* by Jess Stearn. Before reading the biography of Edgar Cayce I had felt uneasy about my clairvoyance. It was a relief to know that another person, Edgar Cayce, saw auras and talked with spirits. Perhaps I needed to explore my gift more, so I decided to try meditation as advised by Edgar Cayce. I started with the candle meditation. It wasn't long before I saw a sea of faces. Since Cayce advised mediators to go higher, I ignored them. Soon I was drifting out of body to a higher and clearer plane where I was greeted by an older gentleman in a wheelchair. He had lost both his legs. He seemed to know me and I sensed that he was a relative. Next to him was a small lady who held a purple flower. "That's my name," she said. When I asked my mother if any of our relatives had lost his legs, she said, "Yes, Grandpa's father had diabetes and lost both legs about a year before he died. He had a housekeeper named Violet who took care of him."

I knew then that I was a medium. However, I still did not feel confident in my abilities, but knew of no place to go for training, so I just studied on my own. I went to the Pyramid bookstore in Cambridge to purchase books on auras, meditation, dreams, and prophecy. Soon, that was all I wanted to read.

In between my occult studies, I worked on an English degree from the University of Massachusetts at Boston. During the summer of 1969, I took a spur of the moment trip to Maine. While having coffee, I spied a two-line notice on the back pages of a Banger newspaper which announced "Camp Etna, open Sunday at 2 p.m." Something stirred within me – call it a hunch or premonition, but I felt I just had to go to Camp Etna.

As soon as I arrived on the grounds, I spied a gray-haired short lady walking around. After chatting with her for a few minutes, I asked, "Do you know any medium who might do a reading today?"

She answered slowly, "Well, if you want an honest reading, see Bill Ellis."

"How do you know him?" I asked.

She smiled sweetly as she answered, "He's my husband."

Rev. Bill Ellis indeed knew a great deal about the spirit world. He could see spirits and identified my grandmother who had died twelve years before. He also saw auras and told me I had a lot of yellow in mind. On my second reading with Rev. Ellis, he looked me in the eye as I was leaving and said, "Someday you will be doing this work."

I thought to myself, "He must tell this to everyone."

As if reading my mind, Rev. Ellis said with emphasis, "I know you don't believe me, but some day you will."

I had the pleasure of meeting Rev. William Ellis one more time. He was in the audience when I did a demonstration of mediumship at Camp Temple Heights in Maine. After the service, I told him the story of how reluctant I was to believe his prediction. We both had a good laugh!

When I looked at the Spiritualist literature that I'd brought home from Camp Etna, I located a development circle in Brookline, Massachusetts, about two miles from my apartment. The circle was run by Rev. Gladys Custance, a trance medium and her husband, Rev. Kenneth Custance, a distinguished silver-haired medium. Both were accomplished harpists, Spiritualist mediums, and ordained ministers. Gladys also had a Hindu guide, the Professor, whose spirit over-shadowed the medium, so she could conduct the classes. I was in the development circle for three years. During this time, I honed my clairsentience, clairvoyance, and clairaudience with the Professor's guidance. The meditations were wonderful, filled with lights and fragrances, as well as messages relayed from the other side.

Finally, on April 23, 1972, I passed my test séance – the final step in becoming a medium. When the date was chosen by the Massachusetts Spiritualist Association of Churches, I was stunned. This date had been on my mind for some time, ever since it had been predicted during an astral travel experience. About three years before, my Hindu guide had taken me on an astral travel trip. Within minutes, I found myself looking down at houses in India. Then I landed in a beautiful pool of turquoise blue water. My Hindu guide, pointed to a newspaper about twenty feet away. "Draw it near with your third eye," he advised. I focused on my third eye and drew the Sunday edition of the *Boston Globe* close enough to read the date – April 23!

Since being certified as a medium by the National Association of Spiritualist Churches, I have served many Spiritualist churches camps, including Lily Dale Assembly in New York. I have also conducted my share of séances, the most notable was the 1997 Official Houdini Séance held at the Goodspeed Opera House in East Haddam, Connecticut. Personally, I believe that Harry Houdini did make a brief appearance at the 1997 Official Houdini Séance when he gave an evidential message to Timothy Gulan, the actor who portrayed him in the play *Metamorphosis*. Alas, his spirit did not return with sufficient strength to open the handcuffs placed on the table which was required as proof.

In addition to performing as a medium, I enjoy teaching others my craft. During summers, I have visited many Spiritualist camps, including Lily Dale. I have done many presentations at Lily Dale including "Dreams and Astral Travel" and "Soul Cycles: Astrology 101." My most recent seminar, "Séance 101," is based on my book on physical mediumship. The Lily Dale audience is most appreciative of my demonstrations of clairvoyance, psychometry, table tipping, and psychic photography.

It is always exciting to go to Lily Dale, whether as a presenter or a visitor. First, as you enter the gates, there is a feeling of peace and spiritual protection. No wonder, for spirit can be seen clairvoyantly all over the grounds. On many occasions, the students from the New England School of Metaphysics have brought their cameras to capture many orb photos. Where else would so many spirits be present?

Lily Dale, by the way, has been a home to many fine mediums, such as Rev. Arthur Ford. When I visited there, I made it a point to take a photograph of Arthur Ford's old home which is now the residence of Dr. Lauren Thibideau. Lily Dale has also been home to many *exceptional* mediums, including Jack Kelly, who was Mae West's psychic. Kelly was known for driving blind-folded, as well as giving evidential messages. Other well-known mediums included Pierre O.L.A. Keeler, the great slate medium, Hazel Riddle, a trumpet medium extraordinaire, and the famous Campbell Brothers, known for the precipitated paintings of

spirit guide Ashur and Abraham Lincoln in the lobby of Maplewood Hotel.

Spirit has also played a role in my writing. While I was putting this book together, more than once, I felt an experienced typist taking over. All of the sudden, words were flowing quickly as my fingers typed a hundred words a minute (double my usual speed) Curious, I made it a point to ask for the names of guides who were assisting when I attended a spirit card séance by Rev. Hoyt Robinette, the amazing physical medium featured in *Séance 101*. I was most pleased to receive this spirit card with the names Carl Hewitt, a Connecticut medium; Rod Serling, creator of the *Twilight Zone*; Clifford Bias, the renowned physical medium; Crazy Horse, an Indian chief;

Precipitated Spirit Cards from Rev. Hoyt Robinette from March 26, 2011

and Phyllis Davis, a psychic artist from Camp Chesterfield, as well as a precipitated picture of the writer who guided me. Of course, it is up to the reader to decide if indeed there is an expert spirit writer assisting.

One

History of Mediumship

Higher Spiritualism is its philosophy, the blending into the one perfect whole of all its parts the union of its phenomena and spirit, the meeting and merging of its body and soul.

~Cora L.V. Tappen Richmond

Mediumship is a universal phenomena. Communication with the dead has been a topic of fascination since time of antiquity to Victorian Spiritualism. Perhaps no civilization has been as preoccupied with death than the ancient Egyptians. They even built huge pyramids so that their kings and queens might pass comfortably into the afterlife. From 2630 BC until 1530 BC, over ninety royal pyramids were constructed – the largest of which is the Great Pyramid of Giza which took over twenty years to complete. It is also unique because it is located at the center of the land mass of the earth and is the most precisely aligned structure of the ancient world. The Great Pyramid is also the only pyramid to have air shafts; one in the King's chamber points to the constellation Orion and a second in the Queen's Chamber points to the star Sirius.

Why such elaborate preparation for death? Clearly the effort – both scientific and financial – would be comparable to that put forth in the United States' space program. It was because death was viewed as a transition to another world, as described in the *Egyptian Book of the Dead*. Here a scene depicts the heart of the dead person being weighed against a feather. Should the deceased be found wanting, his heart would be eaten by the Devourer. If the heart was lighter than a feather, the deceased would be allowed to stay in the pleasant land of reeds.

The ancient Tibetans also had a book describing the afterlife in which one is held accountable for past deeds. *The Tibetan Book of the Death* describes judgment just before rebirth:

> The Lord of Death will say I have looked into the Mirror of
> Karma. So saying he will look into the Mirror of Karma wherein
> every good and evil deed is vividly reflected. Lying will be of
> no avail.[1]

Tibetan Buddhists believe that those who are with us at the time
of death, will be with us in our next life as well. Eventually, through a
succession of incarnations filled with noble deeds, one is able to get off
the wheel of life and remain in the world of spirit.

Mediumship is of prime importance to Tibetan culture. For over
1,300 years, Tibetans have consulted a chief oracle or medium for major state decisions: According to John Vincent Bellezza upper Tibet has
many spirit mediums:

> The spirit-mediums of Upper Tibet, both men and women,
> serve as incarnate forms of the region's most important lha-ri
> (mountain gods), as well as a range of other indigenous deities.
> Traditionally, it is believed that when the thugs (mind) or bla
> (animating principle) of a divinity enters a spirit-medium, it
> variously acts to heal sick people and livestock, exorcise bad
> spirits and harmful influences, bring good fortune, and predict
> the outcome of future events.[2]

The ancient Greeks who believed the departed traveled to a place
called Elysian Fields, also revered their oracles. Some of the best
documented cases of spirit communication come from ancient Greece.
The most noted seer was the Delphi oracle who was usually an older
woman chosen for her high character. She was trained to go into a trance
state and channel the god Apollo. While in a trance, she spoke excitedly
and her ravings were taken down by the priest. The Oracle was consulted
before all major matters of state including wars.

The Oracle or Pythia, as she was called, told Phalanthas, the King of
Sparta, he should delay his invasion of Italy until he felt rain fall from
the sky. When he did not follow the advice, his invasion met with failure.
On second thought, the King of Sparta realized that the message was a
cryptic one. When Phalantha's wife, Aithra, (whose name meant clear
sky) cried, he realized it was time to try another invasion, which was
successful.

The Oracle could also be quite direct. For example, when the Roman
emperor, Nero, consulted her, she cried out, "Your presence defies me.
Be gone matricide; beware of seventy-three!"[3] The thirty-year-old Nero
thought he had another forty-three years to live, but he died the next
year. Seventy-three-year-old Galba succeeded him!

Wealthy Greek citizens not only consulted oracles, but they also
erected monuments and rectangular tombs with elaborate scenes of the

deceased and family members to insure the dead would not be forgotten. Even while family members mourned, they felt assured of an afterlife. For instance:

> Plato taught that before each incarnation, the soul enters into a forgetfulness of that [which has] gone before. The purpose of human learning and philosophy is then to reawake in the soul remembrance of the eternal and spiritual realm of pure forms and ideas.[3]

Not only did the Greeks believe in the spiritual realms, but so did the Hindus and the Buddhists. According to the Upanishads, the soul is trapped in the world of "samsara" (the cycle of death and rebirth) and is compelled to reincarnate until one achieves liberation or "moksha." These sacred texts – the Upanishads, the Bhagavad Gita, and the Brahmans sutras – were taken down by rishis or seers some 3,000 years ago.

The Buddhists accept the principles of Hinduism and assert the goal of life is also liberation from rebirth or Nirvana, which literally means cessation of craving. As long as one is consumed by desire, he will find himself on the wheel of rebirth. Both the Hindus and Buddhist view the afterlife as a series of states some of which are like hell, with the highest state like the Christian concept of heaven.

While reincarnation is not mentioned specifically in the Bible, there are several allusions to this belief which the Essenes, including Jesus, espoused. For example, when the disciples asked Jesus if he was an incarnation of the prophet Elijah, he replied:

> Elijah indeed is to come and will restore all things. But I say to you that Elijah has come already, and they did not know him, but did to him whatever they wished. So also shall the Son of Man suffer at their hand."[4]

Then the disciples understood that he had spoken of John the Baptist.

While John the Baptist and Jesus both suffered, Jesus believed in a world beyond this one. He viewed the afterlife as a comfortable home with many rooms:

> In my Father's house are many rooms; if it were not so, I would have told you. I am going there to prepare a place for you."[5]

References to mediumship are also found in the Bible in both the Old and New Testaments. In the Old Testament, the witch of Endor contacted the spirit of the deceased prophet Samuel at the request of King Saul who wished to question his dead mentor about matters of war.

In the New Testament, the spirits of Elijah and Moses materialized and dematerialized before the eyes of the apostles. As the spirits of Elijah and Moses were seen talking, a cloud came down:

> Then a cloud appeared and enveloped them, and a voice came from the cloud: "This is my Son, whom I love. Listen to him!" Suddenly, when they looked around, they no longer saw anyone with them except Jesus.[6]

While the sight of spirits startled the apostles, spirit visitations were an everyday occurrence for Emanuel Swedenborg (1688 –1772). He claimed that the Lord had opened his Spiritual eyes at 53 so that he could see clearly into the afterlife and talk with spirits. He went on to write over eighteen books on the subject, the best known, *Heaven and Hell*, was published in 1758. The scientist-turned-seer gave this description of the other side of life.

> Life in Spirit is similar to that on the Earth plane, with houses, churches, schools, etc. The process of death is aided by Angels (good spirits); everyone rests for a few days after death and then regains full consciousness.[7]

Eventually, those who are old, sick, or confused regain their health and youth and are allowed to progress to higher levels.

Swedenborg's description of the other side parallels those given by the pioneers of the Spiritualist. In fact, Andrew Jackson Davis (1826-1910) claimed the spirits of Emanuel Swedenborg and the Roman physician Galen as his guides. Not surprisingly, Davis' view of the afterlife bears a strong resemblance to that of Swedenborg. Davis saw the other side as a series of realms, the highest being a place called the Summerland, which according to Andrew Jackson Davis is the highest level, or "sphere," of the afterlife we can hope to enter.[8]

While Rev. Andrew Jackson Davis did much to promote the Spiritualist movement, it actually began in March of 1848 when two young sisters, Kate (7) and Maggie Fox (10), communicated with the spirit of a dead peddler they dubbed Mr. Splitfoot. Soon news of the Fox sisters who communicated with the dead spread throughout of Hydesville, New York. It wasn't long before the press introduced them to larger audiences who were intrigued by the girls as they demonstrated their ability to talk to the spirits through raps. For example, one rap for "yes," two for "no" and three for "maybe." Later, the girls would sit for hours on stage as the spirits rapped out their names with a simple code of one rap for "a," two raps for "b," down the alphabet to twenty-six raps for "z."

Spiritualism gained in popularity during the Civil War. Even President Abraham Lincoln and Mrs. Lincoln invited mediums to the White House.

Medium Nettie Colburn Maynard (1841-1882) claimed the President praised her mediumship with the comment:

> My child, you possess a very singular gift; but that it is of God, I have no doubt. I thank you for coming here tonight. It is more important than perhaps any one present can understand.[9]

Obviously, the President valued Nettie's mediumship which included several levitations of heavy furniture and most important advice from spirit on the Civil War and the Emancipation Proclamation.

Mediumship became increasingly popular during the Victorian era with trance lecturers, such as Cora L. V. (Scott) Tappen (1840–1923). She channeled several books including, *Discourses Through the Mediumship of Mrs. Cora L.V. Tappan,* which is still in print. London-born, Emma Hardinge-Britten (1823–1899) was another excellent stage medium and author. She was active as a trance lecturer, Spiritualist organizer, and author who wrote *Nineteenth Century Miracles: Spirits and Their Work in Every Country of the Earth.*

Thousands were converted to Spiritualism in the United States and England by its early pioneers. Arguably, no group has done more to promote mediumship than the Spiritualists who assert that "the personality of the so-called dead survive the change called death" and that they maintain memories and character when he or she crosses to the afterlife. The group also advocates personal responsibility for progression here and hereafter. While death does not make one responsible, people have the option of changes, including their age. Deceased children, for instance, may choose to grow up on the other side with spirit parents tending to their needs, while an aging grandmother may choose to grow younger. However, when a medium contacts the spirit of your grandmother, she will appear as old and wrinkled as she was in life for the benefit of identification.

While it is not necessary, according to the Spiritualists, for spirit entities to partake of food, spirit may still desire food and drink. Lower spirit even linger in taverns to gratify their desire for alcohol. However, the majority of spirit prefer to spend time with those they loved. Often, they will draw close to this side of life during family celebrations, including the anniversary of their death which Spiritualism views as a new birthday. After death, Spiritualist mediums such as George Anderson and Anne Gehman describe a period of reunions with family and friends on the otherside. Once the deceased gradually adjusts to life on the other side, they will desire to progress through study and service. There are halls of learning on the otherside, ready for those who wish to grow in spirit. Work is often continued. For example, a soul such as Michael Jackson may choose to put on musicals.

Spiritualists abound not only in the United States, but in Brazil where there are an estimated 32 million Spiritists. Like their American counterparts, Brazilian Spiritists believe in the afterlife. Francisco Xavier (1910-2002), Brazil's most cherished medium "psycho scribed" 412 books with his hand guided by spirits such as Emmanuel who had lived in Rome as Senator Publius Lentulus. In Xavier's book, *Nossa Lar*, a group of spirits known collectively as Andre Luiz describe the many realms of the afterlife. These range from places of lofty souls who dwell in peace abodes to the realm of angry spirits who seek dark corners. Those spirits of the higher region are more evolved, and desire to learn and grow spiritually. At the top, there is a higher region of messengers and teachers who can assist those who wish to grow. Apparently, the thoughts and beliefs one has in this world will be the pattern in the next:

> Under these circumstances, once we discarnate, the environment that we will find ourselves in will be full of the mental creations that we lived with while incarnated. Consequently, it's logical that those who thought and talked about nothing else but their illnesses will find themselves enslaved to these thoughts once in the spiritual world.[10]

It is for this reason that there are hospitals on the other side to care for the mentally disturbed and physically ill until they are brought into spiritual awareness.

Shortly after the birth of Spiritualism and Spiritism at the turn of the century, Edgar Cayce, the Sleeping Prophet, began his work. Cayce's guide, known as the Source, continually advised that the present life is only a stage in our evolution. According to Cayce, death is "God's other door."

> Furthermore, people maintain their personalities in the change called death: Do not consider for a moment... that an individual soul-entity passing from earth plane as a Catholic, a Methodist, or an Episcopalian is something else because he is dead! He is only a dead Episcopalian, Catholic, or Methodist.[11]

What does a modern scientist have to say about mediumship? In 2001, Dr. Gary Schwartz began a series of experiments with the nation's top mediums: Anne Gehman, George Anderson, Suzanne Northrop, and Laurie Campbell. Each did two readings: one silent, and one in the which the medium could ask *yes* or *no* questions.

> A very impressive part of this experiment was the mediums' accuracy score, seventy-seven percent during the silent period, compared with eighty-five percent during the *yes/no* questioning period.[12]

The three Fox sisters; from left to right: Margaret, Kate, and Leah

Now that there is more scientific evidence for life after death, what is the best way to make plans for the afterlife? According to Theosophical writer, Geoffrey Hudson:

Each one of us, therefore, is continuously making his after-death conditions by his daily thoughts, motives, feelings, words, and deeds. If we live nobly and beautifully, and unselfishly while on earth, we ensure for ourselves a corresponding measure of happiness in the hereafter.[13]

End Notes

1. W.Y. Evans-Wentz, *The Tibetan Book of the Dead*. Oxford University Press, London, 1960, pages 165-166.
2. www.tibetarchaeology.com/books/.
3. Jeffery Mishlove, *Roots of Consciousness*, Council Oak Books, Tulsa Oklahoma, 1993, page 41.
4. Bible, Matthew 17, verses 10-13.
5. Bible, John 14, verse 2.
6. Bible, Mark 9, verses 4-8.
7. www.fst.org/medium2.htm.
8. Andrew Jackson Davis, *The Great Harmonia*. University of Michigan Press, 1880.
9. Nettie Colburn Maynard, *Was Abraham Lincoln a Spiritualist?* pages 69-73.
10. Chico Xavier, *Nossa Lar*.
11. Hugh Lynn Cayce and Edgar Cayce, *No Death: God's Other Door*, page 111.
12. http://www.afterlife101.com/HESL.html.
13. http://hpb.narod.rugatewaydeath.html/child.

Two

Modern Mediums
and Their Development

And though I have the gift of prophecy, and understand all mysteries,
and all knowledge; and though I have all faith, so that I could remove
mountains, and have not love, I am nothing.

~Holy Bible

While the Delphi Oracle may have been treated like a Hollywood celebrity, the modern medium has her work cut out for her. Until a handful of years ago, many states had laws on the books making fortune telling and mediumship a crime. As recently as 1944, English medium Helen Duncan was arrested for communicating with the dead. She was forced to serve a nine-month sentence when she was found guilty of witchcraft. So many of the pioneers of Spiritualism suffered for their beliefs, that there was once a saying at Camp Chesterfield: "You aren't a real medium unless you have been arrested." Chesterfield's president, Mabel Riffle, was arrested four times but took it all in stride.

Not only have mediums faced persecution by society, but sometimes the mediums themselves are also taken back by their gifts. Bertie Lily Chandler, for example, was afraid of the first spirit she saw at age six. Even if mediums accept their gifts, relatives may ridicule them as "working for the Devil," which happened to Carl Hewitt who grew up in rural North Carolina. While some mediums, such as Clifford Bias, are born with the gift, others such as John Bunker and Estelle Roberts enter the work as adults. Bunker turned to Spiritualism when his young daughter, Eva, died, and Roberts became aware of her clairaudience only after the death of her husband, Hugh.

Contrary to public opinion, most twentieth-century mediums did not become wealthy through their gifts. Many, like Gladys Osborne (1882-1968), charged low fees, and for the poor, no fee at all. As a child,

19

Gladys often saw visions of the other side which she termed "the happy valley." When she was a teenager, she snuck out of her home to attend a Spiritualist meeting in town, where the medium described spirits around the youngster. Later, when she told her mother about the meeting, her mother who was prejudiced about Spiritualism, forbade her daughter to return. A few years later, Gladys was awakened by a vision of her mother floating five feet above her daughter's bed.[1] The young medium was not surprised when she received a telegram the next day from her brother stating: *Mother passed away at two in the morning.*[2]

After her mother died, Gladys tried table tipping with two fellow actresses and an intelligence spelled out the name of Gladys's guide, Feda, her great-great grandmother, a Hindu by birth. Feda used the table to tap out her story: She learned that Feda had been raised by a Scottish family until the age of thirteen, about the year 1800. She married William Hamilton. After the marriage to such a young native, Hamilton was not popular in India and he made arrangements to take Feda back to England. Unfortunately, Feda died in childbirth but her son, Gladys' great-grandfather survived.[3]

Soon Feda became Gladys Osborne's control.

Feda told me that she had been watching over me since I was born, waiting for me to develop my psychic powers so that she could put me into trance... I must confess that the idea of going into a trance did not appeal to me.[4] Despite her misgivings, Gladys did go into a trance and channeled Feda's expansive personality. As she progressed with her mediumship, Gladys Osborne Leonard developed the ability to do proxy readings in which another person would sit on behalf of another, and sometimes Feda would even direct a client to a book in the person's home to find a vital message. Occasionally, cross correspondence would occur in which part of the message would come through Mrs. Leonard and then Feda would give the rest of the message through another sitter.[5]

Gladys Osborne Leonard's most famous séance was one given for Sir Oliver Lodge and Lady Lodge in 1915. The couple received messages from their son, Raymond, who had recently been killed in World War I. The evidential messages from beyond inspired Lodge to write his book, *Raymond, or Life After Death*. Other satisfied investigators included Rev. C. Drayton Thomas, Rev. Vale Owen, James Hewat McKenzie, Mrs. W.H. Salter, and Whately Carrington.

While Gladys Osborne Leonard was drawn to mediumship by childhood visions, Margery Crandon (1888-1941) went into the field on a whim. The wife of wealthy surgeon Dr. Le Roi Goddard Crandon, agreed to try an experiment with table tipping. In May of 1923, the physician and his wife invited two other couples to their home at 10 Lime Street in Boston. Mrs. Crandon, always ready to have fun, thought the whole episode a lark – even though she had recently been told by a tea-room reader that she was psychic. The reader turned out to be correct. Margery was the only one of the six to move the table by supernatural means.

From then on, Dr. Crandon was obsessed with his wife's mediumship. He encouraged her in trance meduimship with good results. Later, Margery used a cabinet for trumpet mediumship. Soon, Mrs. Crandon was channeling the spirit of her dead brother, Walter Stinson, who perished in a train crash in 1911. Walter even came through with direct voice so that everyone in the séance room could hear him! Sitters which included Harvard professors, also witnessed raps, breezes, trance writing in several languages, and apports. While noted researchers, Sir Arthur Conan Doyle and Hereward Carrington praised her mediumship, others such as conjurer Harry Houdini insisted that Margery was a fraud.

About the same time Margery Crandon was practicing mediumship in Boston, Estelle Roberts was a young English widow struggling to raise three children. When her husband, Hugh, died in 1919, he contacted his wife from spirit and requested that she join him. Estelle wisely refused to consider such an idea, but the communication did pique her interest in Spiritualism. When she attended a Spiritualist circle led by Mrs. Elizabeth Cannock, the medium informed the grieving widow that she had the gift of mediumship.[6] When Mrs. Roberts demanded proof from Mrs. Cannock that she had mediumship ability, Estelle Roberts was told to sit at the table. After a few tries, the table levitated and the spirit voice of Red Cloud came through with the message:

> I come to serve the world. You serve with me, and I serve with you.[7]

Since her first meeting with Red Cloud, Estelle Roberts became an exceptional trance medium helping thousands to reach their loved ones.

Of course, not everyone is ready to communicate with the other side; some are shocked by the possibility of life after death. One such sitter, a prim unmarried lady was disturbed to hear the medium tell her that she could see clairvoyantly three men around her – her deceased father and two brothers. Mrs. Roberts tried in vain to reassure her client that these spirits visited her at night. The spinster replied:

> Mrs. Roberts, if Spiritualism teaches that male spirits can come into one's room after one has retired, I want nothing more to do with it![8]

A contemporary of Estelle Roberts, Helen Duncan (1897-1956), also caused quite a stir when she materialized spirits during World War II when Duncan's services were much in demand – a sailor materialized to tell his mother that his ship, HMS *Barham*, had recently been sunk. The British

Admiralty were furious at what they considered a breach of security, so they found an archaic law – Witchcraft Act 1735 – and arrested Helen Duncan. Forty-one witnesses testified on her behalf, including Air Force officer, Wing Commander George Mackie who stated that he had seen his deceased father and mother materialize at one of Helen Duncan's séances.[9] Mary Blackwell, President of the Pathfinder Spiritualist Society, stated that she had attended over a hundred such materialization séances and that she saw fifteen or more spirits materialize – each one conversing with their relatives in their native tongues of "French, German, Dutch, Welsh, Scottish, and Arabic."[10]

Another woman, Kathleen McNeill, told how her sister had appeared at a séance with the medium: Her sister had died previously after an operation, and the news of her death could not have been known. Yet Albert, Helen Duncan's guide, announced she had just passed over. Sadly, even with such extraordinary testimony, the mother of six was found guilty and imprisoned at Holloway prison for nine months. As she was led away, Helen Duncan protested in her Scottish accent:

> I never hee'd so mony a lies in a my life.[11]

Just as noted medium, Helen Duncan, saw spirits even as a small child in Scotland, Eileen Garrett saw spirit children as a small child in Ireland which gave the orphaned medium a sense of comfort. Later, as her psychic gifts unfolded, she sought advice from Mrs. Kelway Bamber who helped her with trance and was instrumental in linking the young medium to her first guide, Uvani. Mrs. Bamber also introduced Eileen Garrett (1893-1970) to many esoteric groups around London, including the British College of Psychic Science. Mr. and Mrs. McKenzie, the founders of the college, believed that mediumship was a tool that could be used to investigate levels of "perception and consciousness."[12]

Both McKenzies helped Eileen Garrett work to deepen her trance state connection with her Oriental guide. He (McKenzie) explained that a control personality is only the interpreter of what reaches him from the other states of consciousness, and, therefore, each control has to be taught to make the purest use of its powers and transmit the highest truth available to it.[13] Eileen J. Garrett was not only a research subject at the British College of Psychic Science in London, but also in the United States at Duke University under the eye of its director, Dr. J. B. Rhine. In 1951, Eileen Garret founded her own research group, the Parapsychology Foundation in New York City. Several fine mediums have made America their home, such as Arthur Ford, Clifford Bias, Mable Riffle, Mamie Schultz Brown, Anne Gehman, Brian Hurst, Carl Hewitt, James Van Praagh, and Hoyt Robinette.

Perhaps the best known of the American mediums is Rev. Arthur Ford (1897-1971) who became aware of his gift while serving in the

Army in 1918. Often he would clairaudiently hear the names of soldiers who were going to die from Spanish flu. Within days, the names he heard would be listed on the casualty report in the exact order Ford was told by the spirit voice. After the war, he became a Spiritualist, around 1921, and he soon developed the gift of trance mediumship with the spirit of Fletcher, a French Canadian young man who had died during World War I, as his control. In 1927, Ford traveled to England where he gave very evidential mediumship readings to total strangers in the audience. Often he gave both firsthand last names. Sir Arthur Conan Doyle was so taken with Ford's mediumship that he praised Ford as the most amazing medium he had seen in forty-one years.[14] When Doyle advised Ford to make mediumship his life's work, Arthur Ford took the advice. He credited Paramahansa Yogananda for his deep trance abilities. Apparently, the guru taught Ford methods of conscious projection. In 1965, Ford explained his trance mediumship as follows:

> In my case, I go to sleep because I was trained by a yoga, in this state of unconsciousness in which my objective mind is pushed aside; there is a personality called Fletcher who comes through.[15]

Rev. Arthur Ford went on to become a very well-known medium. His most famous séances were for Bess Houdini, Rev. Sun Myung Moon, and for Bishop Pike, which was the first televised séance in Canada. Mrs. Houdini, was so happy with the evidence brought through, she wrote a letter verifying the fact that the spirit of her late husband, Harry Houdini, had indeed returned through the mediumship of Ford. In November 1964, he conducted two lengthy séances for Sun Myung Moon. Later, in 1967, Arthur Ford gained national attention when he conducted the first séance on television during which he made contact with Jim, deceased son of Bishop James Pike. Arthur Ford had as many challenges as successes. In 1949, he suffered a breakdown due to alcoholism. Fletcher stopped working with Arthur Ford because of Ford's addiction, but the guide returned in the 1950s. Arthur Ford publicly credited Alcoholics Anonymous for his recovery, and by 1956, Arthur Ford became one of the founders of Spiritual Frontier Fellowship.

While Arthur Ford was best known for his trance mediumship, Mable Riffle was known for her physical mediumship. The Midwestern medium faced arrest four times for charges of humbuggery and fraud. Faithful to her spirit teacher, Dr. Henry Williams, Rev. Riffle did not complain:

> I do not mind being arrested for I feel I am no better than thousands who have gone through hell to prove to this that man survives the change called death.[16]

Mable Riffle was a gifted clairvoyant, clairaudient, trance medium, billet reader, and trumpet medium. She credits her spirit teacher Dr. Henry Williams for her development. He instructed her early on to use her band of guides, which included an Oriental, a Hindu, an American Indian, as well as a guide for inspiration, a child page.[17] Mable Riffle also advised her students to relax. She advocated simple stretching exercises to relax the body.

John Bunker, another Chesterfield medium, concurs with Mable Riffle that relaxation is the key development. He sat for development with the medium Margaret Bright. In this class, his only daughter, Eva, who passed into spirit when she was ten, would be his messenger. She worked with him in that capacity until the development of his apport mediumship. As Bunker's trumpet mediumship and reputation grew, he was consulted by many well-known figures, including the "veiled lady" who visited Rudolf Valentino's grave each year. On the anniversary of Valentino's death, a beautiful lady arrived for a trumpet mediumship session in which spirit speaks through the trumpet so the sitter can talk with the deceased.

A man spoke through the trumpet and, suddenly, Bunker realized it was Rudolf Valentino. He was talking to the "veiled lady"![18]

Even more evidential than hearing the voice of a loved one, is the sight of a materialized spirit.

One excellent materialization medium, Bertie Lily Chandler, was initially shy of the first spirit she saw at six. Later, she learned she was a natural trance medium during a Spiritualist circle in 1918. At her third visit, she spontaneously went in to trance! In addition to trance mediums, Bertie Lily Chandler became a fine materialization medium at Camp Chesterfield. She followed the tenets of the Master Jesus and believed in plenty of exercise in the fresh air. She also believed that there are "many master souls who are looking for an instrument of high purpose and character."[19] William Pelly gave an account of a materialization séance of Bertie Chandler that he witnessed in Indianapolis in May of 1941. As the gracious medium slept in her spirit cabinet, several figures appeared including Harriet, Pelly's first child born in November 1912 who succumbed to cerebral meningitis at age two. Pelly saw a mound of ectoplasm build up in the room and his daughter materialized as a young woman before his eyes.[20] Even more amazing, the spirit of his daughter greeted her brother William and sister Adelaine who were present. After the greeting, Harriet asked for her father's handkerchief and "began tugging at the fabric increasing its size as a towel to the size of a bed sheet." When her curious father asked how she accomplished the feat, Harriet replied:

> I'm increasing the distances – by the Power of Thought – between each electron and proton in the linen's Atoms.[21]

Perhaps the best known of the physical medium at Camp Chesterfield was Rev. Clifford Bias. He became famous for his trumpet mediumship and precipitated spirit cards. The medium even wrote a book on the subject physical mediumship in which he advised students to sit for mental mediumship first, before attempting physical phenomena. Rev. Bias was also an ardent Spiritualist and one of the founders of the Universal Spiritualist Association.

While Clifford Bias's family seemed to accept his gift, Mamie Schultz Brown had a Catholic mother who was dead set against mediums. When her father died, he came through a séance to encourage his daughter in her gift of mediumship. She began development in 1914, and a few years later, she became well known for her ability to do blindfold billet readings. She advised the billet medium to sense, hear, and see spirit as they hold the small slip of paper in their hands.

> Of course, billet reading can be done from psychometric and inspiration alone, but it is much more effective when combined with the other phases.[22]

Robert G. Chaney also was known for his billet readings, as well as trumpet séances in red light, and spirit photography at Camp Chesterfield. Chaney had a family background in Spiritualism through his psychic great-grandmother. Chaney sat for six weeks for development before he heard a spirit voice say, "Grandmother Holcomb."[23] Soon he was doing reading for others. Eventually, he developed trumpet mediumship and psychic photography. Chaney stressed the importance of tuning into spirit before placing the sensitive side of photography paper over the solar plexus. He learned the gift from spirit during a trumpet séance when a picture of a young man materialized.

Rev. Robert Chaney was fortunate that his parents believed in Spiritualism. Such was not the case for Rev. Carl Hewitt who grew up in North Carolina, a small rural community. Throughout his childhood, Carl was shunned, because the psychic phenomena and mediumship were believed to be the work of the devil. People did not appreciate it when the young medium, at 4, predicted his sister Annie's death. Since so many family members made fun of Carl's abilities, he did not persue his mediumship until he was living in Connecticut and was a successful businessman. One night, while working in his Gales Ferry beauty salon, a friend invited Carl Hewitt to a nearby Spiritualist church. *How can I possibly go?* he thought. *It is Thursday night and I have four appointments.* Spirit had other plans, and one by one each patron called to cancel. He was glad he attended this Spiritualist meeting where a medium described Carl's life, and even told him he had the ability to be a spirit messenger and that "one day, he would stand before large audiences delivering Spirit messages."[24] The message came true in 1974 when Carl Hewitt was ordained as a spiritualist minister and had been credited with predicting credit cards, plasma TVs, the whereabouts of runaway children, and the election of Jimmy Carter; and he is on Record with NYS predicting a terrorist attack on the Statue of Liberty.[24] One of the most touching events for Hewitt was the spirit of his brother-in-law which came though a medium at Camp Etna to apologize profusely for ridiculing the sensitive medium!

Another medium, Anne Gehman, also faced persecution by family members. The talented lady grew up in an Amish household, and at 12 was confirmed in the Mennonite faith. However, she was still plagued with dreams and visions that she could not share with her family. As her life became increasingly difficult, she was at an emotional crossroads. Was life worth living? Fate stepped in to answer that question. The despondent young woman went for a drive, and suddenly her Studebaker, which never gave her any trouble, stalled in front of a house in Cassadaga, Florida. She knocked on the door of the owner, Wilbur Hull. The white-haired kindly gentleman invited her inside. "I don't know who you are," he said, "but they told me you were coming.[25] Wilbur told the young woman that there was a Spiritualist Camp – Camp Cassadaga. After he explained how Spiritualists believed in communication with the dead, Wilbur handed Anne his ring for psychometry and she immediately picked up on a spirit – Rose. While Anne had experienced the presence of spirits before, for the first time she had someone to validate her gift. Soon Anne was sitting in Wilbur Hull's developmental circle and later became a minister and one of Cassadaga's top mediums.

Rev. Gehman had many adventures in mediumship. Perhaps the most touching involves her only child. Anne had been told by her doctors that she could not have children, however, another medium saw her going on a trip to Brazil, and predicted a pregnancy. Anne felt it was just a wishful thing. Later, when Anne and her husband took a trip to Brazil, she made it a point to see the psychic surgeons for a healing treatment. When she returned to the United States, she was overjoyed to find out she was pregnant with Rhoda!

While Anne Gehman trained at Camp Casssadaga in Florida, British medium, Brian Hurst, received his mediumship training at the College of Psychic Sciences in Kensington, England. The young drama student found the college a fascinating place with its walls displaying portraits of the pioneers of psychic research.

The college also sponsored excellent lecturers, including Lord and Lady Dowling, Brigadier Firebrace, and Ann Copley. As with many fledging mediums, Brian Hurst lacked confidence in his abilities. Mrs. Copley, a veteran physical medium, and her husband, Bob, became Hurst's mentors, along with noted medium, Leslie Flint. Appalled by the jealousy among mediums (which continues to be a problem with today's workers), he made a sincere effort to be positive. "There is no doubt that all of us on the spiritual path do need to watch our environment, our

The ill-fated Dirigible *R101*

associations, our thoughts, and our actions."[26]

In his book, *Heaven Can Help*, Brian Hurst gives an honest account of his early years as a medium, travel to India, investigation into psychic surgery, and conversations with spirits during trumpet séances. One memorable episode occurred during a trumpet séance with Jim Hutchings. Brian Hurst, as well as others in the room, heard the distinctive voice of Brian's deceased Aunt Mary coming out of the trumpet. His aunt said:

> I have a lovely house over here. You should see the flowers in my garden. The hollyhocks are even taller than the ones at the bungalow.[27]

The message was especially significant to her nephew as he used to pick hollyhocks in front of her home. At the close of the séance, Aunt Mary urged him to let others know the truth about life after death.

When Brian Hurst relocated to California in 1980, he attracted many students, including James Van Praagh, who was working in the legal department of Paramount Studios at the time. A colleague at his workplace invited him to visit Spiritualist medium Brian Hurst who told him that one day he would be a medium. He was intrigued enough with the prediction that he began to pick up books on psychic development and find ways to hone his skills. Brian Hurst's prediction came true when James Van Praagh went on to become a nationally known medium in 1997 with the publication of his book, *Talking to Heaven*.

End Notes

1. www.fst.org/leonard.htm.
2. Suzy Smith, *She Spoke to the Dead*, Mass Markets Books, 1972, page 23.
3. Suzy Smith, *She Spoke to the Dead*, Mass Markets Books, 1972, page 33.
4. www.fst.org/leonard.htm/.
5. www.fst.org/leonard.htm/.
6. *Fifty Years a Medium*, by Estelle Roberts (www.spiritwritings.com).
7. *Fifty Years a Medium*, by Estelle Roberts (www.spiritwritings.com).
8. *Fifty Years a Medium*, by Estelle Roberts (www.spiritwritings.com).
9. www.helenduncan.org.uk/helenstory/witchtrial.html.
10. www.helenduncan.org.uk/helenstory/witchtrial.html.
11. www.helenduncan.org.uk/helenstory/witchtrial.html.
12. www.fst.org/garrett.htm.
13. *Eileen Garrett, Adventures in the Supernormal*, Helix Press, New York, NY 2002, p. 95.
14. http://en.wikipedia.org/wiki/Arthur_Ford.
15. *Nothing So Strange: The Autobiography of Arthur Ford by Arthur Ford* in collaboration with Marguerite Harmon Bro, Harper & Row, 1958.
16. Robert G. Chaney, *Mediums and the Development of Mediumship* Psychic Books, Eaton Rapids MI,1946, pages 79-80.
17. Robert G. Chaney, *Mediums and the Development of Mediumship* Psychic Books, Eaton Rapids MI, 1946, page 80.
18. Robert G. Chaney, *Mediums and the Development of Mediumship* Psychic Books, Eaton Rapids MI,1946, page 89.
19. Robert G. Chaney, *Mediums and the Development of Mediumship* Psychic Books, Eaton Rapids MI,1946, page 208.
20. www.sanctugermanus.net/ebooks/Why%201%20Believe%20 th%Dead%20are%20Alive%20Pelleypdf.
21. www.sanctugermanus.net/ebooks/Why%201%20Believe%20 th%Dead%20are%20Alive%20Pelleypdf
22. Robert G. Chaney, *Mediums and the Development of Mediumship* Psychic Books, Eaton Rapids MI,1946.
23. www.gotsc.org/carl.htm.
24. www.gotsc.org/carl.htm.
25. Anne B. Gehman and Wayne Knoll, *The Priest and the Medium*. Hay House, 2009, page 45.
26. Brian Hurst, *Heaven Can Help*, iUniverse, Lincoln, 2001, page 105.
27. www.answers.com/topic/james-van-prasgRead.

Three

Science Examines the Afterlife

The intuitive mind is a sacred gift and the rational mind is a faithful servant. We have created a society that honors the servant and has forgotten the gift.

~ Albert Einstein

Scientists from Dr. Gary Swartz to Professor William James have studied mediums with a logical eye. While Dr. Freud was formulating personality theories of the id, ego, and superego in Vienna, Dr. William James was studying mediumship and varieties of religious experiences in the United States. James, who formulated the theory of "states of consciousness," believed in the world beyond, as did Dr. Carl Jung, a protégé of Freud's, who did his doctoral dissertation on mediumship. Jung eventually broke with Freud when Jung refused to view the libido as purely sexual. Dr. Jung continued to research the mystical and write on synchronicity, The Golden Flower, I Ching, and dreams. While Jung did not formally research the phenomena in a laboratory, his investigation into the mystical added much to the field.

One of the first scientists to study mediumship was eminent physicist, William Crookes, who also investigated the physical medium, Daniel Douglas Home (1833-1886). Home, who was born in Scotland, emigrated to the United States where he lived in New London, Connecticut, with his aunt, a non-believer. When raps began in the house, the aunt threw him out because she believed the psychic phenomena to be the work of the devil.

D.D. Home had many unusual psychic abilities. He could not only produce raps, but levitate objects, and had the ability of handling hot coals without injuring himself. His most remarkable gift was that of levitation in broad daylight. Fortunately for Home, others such as Judge John Edmunds of the New York State Supreme Court; and Robert Hare, professor of chemistry at the University of Pennsylvania; England's Lord Adare, the poetess; Elizabeth Barrett Browning; and Dr. William Crookes believed his powers to be beneficial.

Dr. Crookes invited D.D. Home to his laboratory to test the stories about music by spirits. Crookes designed a cage with room for only one hand to enter. Inside the cage he placed an accordion. Under these strict test conditions, D.D. Home was able to affect the accordion. William Crookes made this report when he saw an accordian move without human fingers on the keys:

> Very soon the accordion was seen by those on either side to be waving about in a somewhat curious manner; then sounds came from it and finally notes were played in succession.[1]

Even more evidential, the accordion continued to play after Home's let go of his thumb and middle finger with no person touching it!

Dr. William Crookes' most amazing experiments were with a medium by the name of Florence Cook whose ability to materialize spirits had caused a sensation among Spiritualists. For over three years, Crooks attended séances with Florence Cook in which he saw her most famous spirit, Katie King. He also took over forty photographs, even photographing Florence Cook and the spirit together. Crookes carefully conducted his session with the medium to avoid any fraud:

> I prepare and arrange my library myself as the dark cabinet, and usually, after Miss Cook has been dining and conversing with us, and scarcely out of our sight for a minute, she walks directly into the cabinet, and I, at her request, lock its second door, and keep possession of the key all through the séance.[2]

This spirit child appeared to be solid, and that a doctor was able to pick up pulse and another sitter felt the spirit child's weight when she sat on his lap. Was it extraordinary mediumship or outright fakery? From the multitude of accounts from other sitters and the photographs of the spirit child, it would seem from all accounts to be genuine at the time. Later, when Crookes' interest in the medium was discovered, his critics claimed the studies were unscientific. Still, Crookes left a remarkable amount of photographic evidence to prove his case.

The first formal society to study paranormal, the Society for Psychical Research was founded in London in 1882. Henry Sidgwick, a Cambridge moral philosopher with a reputation for skepticism was chosen as its first director. Thought transference, mesmerism, psychic emanations, physical phenomena, and haunted houses were chosen for research. The society became intrigued with an Italian woman, Eusapia Palladino, a peasant from Naples, known for her unusual telekinetic abilities. In trance, her control, the spirit John King, would come through levitating tables, ringing bells, and materializing small objects.

French researcher, Charles Richet was so taken with the medium, that he invited Palladino to his private island to conduct a séance, in 1894, at the Sir Oliver Lodge. Charles Richet and F.W. H. Myers also attended and Lodge gave this report to the Society for Psychical Research:

> 12:49: A small cigar box fell onto our table, and a sound was heard in the air of something rapping. R (Richet) was holding head and right hand. M (Myers) was holding left hand, raised it in the air, holding it lightly by the tips of his fingers, with part of his own free hand. A saucer containing small shot, from another part of the room was then put in the hand of M in the air. A covered wire of the electric battery came unto the table and wrapped itself around R's and E's (Eusapia's) hand and was pulled until E. called out.[3]

Both Lodge and Myers were so impressed by Eusapia Palladino's abilities and were planning to bring her to England for further testing. Unfortunately, her abilities went into decline and her séances became chaotic so that further testing was impossible.

While Eusapia was primarily a physical medium, another excellent mental medium, Lenora Piper, was studied with more favorable results by William James and Edward Fielding. Fielding wrote in 1908:

> I have seen this extraordinary woman, sitting visible outside the curtain, held hand and foot by my colleagues while some entity within the curtain has over and over again pressed my hand in a position clearly beyond her reach.[4]

The Society also investigated English medium Gladys Osborne Leonard with favorable results. Leonard, known as a mental medium, under the direction of her spirit guide Feda, a Hindu girl who died in child birth at 14. Sir Oliver Lodge was very impressed by her reading:

> According to Leonard herself, it was the spring of 1914 that Feda announced that something big and terrible was going to happen in the world and that through Mrs. Leonard she would have to help many people. This prediction came true with the outbreak of World War I. Mrs. Leonard's mediumship was very much in demand by those such as Sir Oliver

Professor William James

Lodge who lost his son, Raymond, in September 1915.

When Lodge visited the medium, he was happy to communicate with his son.

> "At a subsequent sitting with Mrs. Leonard, Raymond via Feda, who appeared to communicate and spoke at some length about some group photographs that had been taken of his company. At that point Lodge had not received the photographs, but when they arrived, they confirm the details to which the 'Raymond Communicator' had drawn to his attentions."[5]

Later the American Society of Psychical Research studied Margery Crandon, whose control was her deceased bother, Walter, produced some unusual phenomena including direct voice:

> Walter, so it seems, was even able, on one occasion, to penetrate a sound-proof box so as to activate a microphone which it enclosed, whence his voice was relayed to sitters in another room.[6]

Margery Crandon also had the ability, while in trance, to produce fingerprints of spirit on a wax pad. Dr. R.J. Tillyard who had a private sitting with Margery Crandon on August 10, 1928, made these observations:

> During the séance, first of all thumb marks, whose markings did not resemble the thumb marks of either of the two present, were obtained on various pieces of soft wax, and later in the séance an independent voice claiming to be the medium's brother, carried on an animated conversation with Dr. Tillyard.[7]

In 1927, Dr. J.B. Rhine began his systematic study of the paranormal at Duke University intrigued by the claims of a young gambler that he could influence the outcome of the dice. Rhine began his experiments in psychokinesis (PK), the ability for mind to influence matter. He continued his studies at Duke University for forty years. Early studies in PK were very successful and able to be duplicated by other researchers using coins, cubes, marbles, and other targets. One of Rhine's best subjects was a divinity student, Herbert Pearce, who averaged 9.7 hits in some 90 consecutive runs.[8]

The experiments also indicated a correlation between PK and ESP:

> So far then, PK and ESP seemed to share common characteristics they did not at face value conform to physical lawfulness, showed marked decline effects, and the subjects successful at one could achieve success at the other.[9]

Dr. Rhine was able to research the gifted medium and clairvoyant, Eileen Garrett. At first she found the ESP test difficult until the symbols were transmitted through a sender.

> On the other hand, in working on the clairvoyance test with Dr. Rhine, I discovered that by being passed though the mind of another (person), the symbols came alive. My scores rose perceptibly. In the telepathy experiments, I was freed from direct concentration on the cards themselves and was able to receive the symbols from the mind of the transmitter, where they acquired vitality and provided energy for the stimulus to work.[10]

In other words, using a person to transmit the symbols enabled Eileen Garrett to utilize her clairvoyance to read them.

Western scientists were also able to study Uri Geller's talent when Dr. Andrija Puharich arranged for Geller to be tested at the Sandford Research Institute in Menlo Park, California. In 1973, Dr. Russell Targ watched carefully as Geller demonstrated the ability to bend objects and to germinate seeds. He also impressed Dr. Thelma Moss, a UCLA professor when she tested Uri's "watch-fixing and metal-bending abilities." Geller is known also for his amazing ability to bend spoons by simply holding one in his hands. Professor Gerald Schroeder's description is typical of those given by other scientists:

> The one he bent with me preening over his shoulder continued to bend even after he placed it on the ground and stepped away.[11]

Uri Geller was unusual in another way. Apparently just watching his performance had an effect on the psychic abilities of some of the television audience:

> Many people reported experiencing unusual visual or telepathic phenomena and several reported that, after watching Geller's demonstrations, they also were able to produce various psychokinetic effects. On occasions when I have broadcast radio interviews with Uri, dozens of listeners have reported psychokinetic phenomena in their own homes.[12]

Dr. Russell Targ conducted many experiments with other gifted psychics in addition to Uri Geller. From his studies of quantum physics, Targ developed experiments in remote viewing. According to Ingo Swan, one of the "remote viewers" utilized, most of the work was done by "ordinary people" who were trying remote viewing for the first time:

> Remote viewing is an amalgam of what used to be called thought
> transference, telepathy, and clairvoyance. It is a process whereby a
> viewer (formerly a subject or the sensitive) perceives information
> about a distant location and tries to describe the location, often
> in great detail before the location is known to him.[13]

Ingo Swan, Joseph McGoneagle and Sean David Morton demonstrate considerable talent in remote viewing today.

In 1991, Dr. Arthur Hastings, author of *With the Tongues of Men and Angels,* believes channeled material should also be examined more seriously by scientists:

> What we call channeling today draws on an age-old process to
> communicate messages beyond the individual ego.[14]

He goes on to point out many religious mainstream institutions have come from these channeled teachings. Dr. Hastings recommends more study of the Biblical prophecies: Jane Roberts's *The Nature of Personal Reality, A Course in Miracles*, the poetry and literature of William Blake; as well as Jon Klimo's book, *Channeling;* and his own book, *With the Tongues of Men and Angels.*

Other researchers have worked on authenticating mediumship. In 2001, Dr. Gary Swartz and Dr. Linda Russek experimented with two mediums. Their question: Can mediums receive accurate information under laboratory conditions? The results showed an eighty-three percent accuracy for the actual readings which gave details on both the living and deceased. While some of the information obtained was general, the bulk of information was deemed precise. The readings, dubbed the "White Crow" Readings, appear in *The Journal of the Society of Psychical Research.*

In addition to mediums, ordinary people have experienced the life-after-death communications. According to a 1983 Gallup Poll, approximately five percent of the population has had some type of near-death experience (NDE). Dr. Raymond Moody who studied 150 such people found 15 common characteristics which he discusses in his book, *Life after Life.* For example, most people report hearing a buzzing sound or a loud ring, feeling a pull out of their bodies and going through a tunnel of light. At the end of the tunnel they see the spirits of deceased loved ones waiting for them. At some point, they are told to return to their bodies or they feel a strong desire to return for unfinished family responsibilities. However, they return with a change of consciousness and a firm belief that there is no death. They also have greater compassion for their fellow man and thirst for higher knowledge.

When Betty Bland, President of the Theosophical Society in America, 2002-2011, had her near-death experience, she was transported to what she describes as a "Council of Light," a group of enlightened but formless beings filled with light. With the help of the Council, Bland perceived "threads to past and future" where "successes were viewed as completions and short comings relegated to futures lives."[15] Betty Bland was advised, "I had accomplished all that was necessary for this life." Her near-death episode however, left her with a desire to fulfill her potential with a strong tendency "to actualizing and to increasing a sense of purpose."[16]

Unable to find a satisfactory explanation in traditional literature, Bland turned to theosophical books. It wasn't long before Betty Bland became a very active member in the Theosophical Society of America, eventually becoming its national president 2002 – 2011.

Not only do those who survive death become more spiritually attuned, some survivors also return with psychic abilities. Such was the case for Dannion Brinkley (1950). The author of *Saved by the Light* was struck by lightning on September 17, 1975. While out of his body, the tough Marine met "beings of light" who showed him boxes that they inserted into a television to Brinkley's surprise. He saw a man with the initials R.R. becoming President in 1980, the 1986 Chernoble nuclear power plant explosion, the Desert Storm war, as well as the collapse of the Soviet Union. When he asked about the future, the beings of light told him: "Watch the Soviet Union. How the Russian people go, so goes the world. What happens to Russia is the basis for everything that will happen to the economy of the free world."[17]

In 1991, Pam Reynolds Lowery (1956 – May 22, 2010) had her near-death experience under medical supervision to correct an aneurysm. Her only chance of survival was a rare seven-hour operation which included a one-hour procedure known as a standstill operation. During this procedure, Reynolds' body temperature was lowered to 60 °F (16 °C), her breathing and heartbeat were stopped and the blood was cleared from her head in order to treat the aneurysm. While Reynolds was in the "standstill," the Atlanta singer heard a sound like D natural that seemed to pull her out of her body.

> As I listened to the sound, I felt it was pulling me out of the top of my head. The further out of my body I got, the more clear the tone became. I had the impression it was like a road, a frequency that you go on.[18]

Then she went through "a tunnel vortex" and at one point heard her grandmother calling her. As she entered a very bright light, she saw her grandmother, Uncle Gene, and her great-great-Aunt Maggie greeted her, as well as other people she did not recognize.

> It was communicated to me – that's the best way I know how to say it, because they didn't speak like I'm speaking – that if I went all the way into the light something would happen to me physically. They would be unable to put *this* me back into the *body* me, like I had gone too far and they couldn't connect.[19]

Eventually, her Uncle Gene pushed her back into her body which she described as like "diving into a pool of ice water."

Her cardiologist, Dr. Michael Sabom wrote a book on Pam Reynolds who later died of a heart condition in 2010. His book, *Light and Death,* gives a detailed timeline of all the events that occurred along with Pam Reynolds's own experiences. Dr. Peter Fenwich, a neuropsychiatrist who has examined near-death experiences, believes they are real, but is at a loss to give a scientific explanation. Dr. Fenwick concluded that it remains a puzzle for society:

> This is a puzzle for science. I have not yet seen any good scientific explanation which can explain this fact.[20]

End Notes

1. 1871 *Quarterly Journal of Science*, Royal Society of Science.
2. www.williamjames.com/Folklore/MINDOVER.htm.
3. *Quarterly Journal of Science.* Royal Society of Science.
4. John Beloff, *Parapsychology, A Concise History*, 1993, St. Matin's Press NY, page 121.
5. John Beloff, *Parapsychology, A Concise History,* 1993, St. Matin's Press NY, page 110.
6. Arthur Findlay, *On the Edge of the Etheric*, SNU publications, 1951, page 30.
7. J.B. Rhine, *Extra-Sensory Perception* 1934-1964-9173 (Chapter Seven).
8. Scott Rogo, *Parapsychology: A Century of Inquiry*, Dell Publishing, New York, 1973, page 216.
9. Eileen J. Garrett, *Adventures in the Supernormal*, Helix Press, New York, N.Y. 2002, page 116.
10. John Beloff, *Parapsychology, A Concise History*, 1993, St. Martin's Press New York, pages 182-183.
11. www.williamjames.com/Folklore/MINDOVER.htm.
12. www.williamjames.com/Folklore/MINDOVER.htm.
13. Charles Tart, editor, *Body, Mind, Spirit.* Hampton Roads Publishing Company, Charlottesville, VA,1997, page 95 and 211.
14. John Beloff, *Parapsychology, A Concise History*, 1993, St. Matin's Press New York, page 121.
15. www.theosophical.org/publications/quest-magazine/1210.
16. www.theosophical.org/publications/quest-magazine/1210.
17. Dannion Brinkley, *Saved by the Light*, HarperTorch 1995.
18. www.near-death.com/experiences/evidence01.html.
19. www.near-death.com/experiences/evidence01.html.
20. www.near-death.com/experiences/evidence01.html.

Four

Natural Law

Life is not chance, accident, or even coincidence. The whole of life is governed by immutable natural law.

~Silver Birch

While a scientist studies the laws of physics, a medium studies the Divine laws that transcend those of the physical universe. The Divine laws do not belong to any one country or religion, but work progressively for the good of humanity. If one wishes to develop his/her gift of spirit communication, knowledge of natural law is essential.

What exactly is natural law? Andrew Jackson Davis taught that natural laws "were established by one great positive mind" and that "every particle of matter possesses the same power which governs the whole universe and in which particles you see a representation of the Divine laws.[1] In other words, as above, so below.

Another author, Henry Drummond (1851-1897), explained that natural law governs both the physical and spiritual world and "must be applied to all aspects of life and that they do not operate under one set of principles in the natural world and another set in the spiritual."[2] Drummond, a gifted evangelist who was an ordained minister, became famous in 1874 with his work, *The Greatest Thing in the World*, which is about the Law of Love. Later, in 1883, Henry Drummond wrote his classic, *Natural Law in the Spiritual World*.

According to Andrew Jackson Davis, Henry Drummond, and other Spiritualist writers, there are many natural laws. Chief among them are the Golden Rule, the Law of Karma, the Law of Attraction, the Law of Thought, the Law of Compensation, the Law of Continuity, the Law of Abundance, the Law of Love, and the Law of Harmony.

Over 2,000 years ago, Jesus the Christ taught the Golden Rule: "Do unto others as you would have them do unto you" – this same idea is stated in other religions. The Buddhists, for instance, note: "One should seek for others the happiness one desires for himself." The Hebrews also believe "Whatsoever you do not wish your neighbor to do to you, do not unto him." If society made an effort to live by the Golden Rule, war, famine, and crime would be eradicated, for how could anyone kill, starve, or batter his fellow man, if he knew he was killing, starving, or battering himself?

How does the Golden Rule work? It operates through the Law of Karma. In the Bible it is stated "as a man sows, so shall he reap." Thus, if an individual commits good deeds, good will return. However, if the individual chooses to harm others, he or she will have to pay the consequence. Karma is like a pendulum set in motion. As Aristotle stated many years ago, "Even God cannot change the past."

Dr. Douglas Baker points out the karma of the alcoholic may often be the need for power. Instead of being powerful and admired, the addict now becomes the object of scorn, as all eyes are upon him/her. Until, the addict learns to look within for strength, the thirst for power (and alcohol) will not be quenched.

Nations have karmas, too. For example, clairvoyant, C.W. Leadbeater saw the United States as a reincarnation of the Byzantine Empire which existed from 306 AD to 1453 AD. While at its height of economic and military power, civil strife weakened the nation. By the fifteenth century, the once-powerful empire collapsed when the Muslins conquered Constantinople. Today Byzantium has become synonymous with decadence, a trait not unlike that of Hollywood.

While the past cannot be changed, future karma can be altered by present thought and action. The Bible teaches "think and you shall be." For example, the more positive thoughts one thinks, the more positive his or her life becomes. It is through the law of attraction one can attract right relationship or right livelihood. Buddhists believe Sangha, right relationship, is part of the three jewels of Buddhist practice – Buddha (the Divine), Dharma (duty), and Sangha (community). The same is true for mediumship. If you wish to become a strong medium, then practice time with the Divine through meditation, and spiritual community. It is through spiritual practices and fulfilling your individual duties of life that a medium attracts powerful spiritual allies.

In fact, the Law of Thought is most important in the development of spirit communication. An interesting example of this is the case of channeler, J.Z. Knight. Her guide, Ramtha, monitored her thoughts for several years before she became a channel for the Ram. At one point in her development, she had a judgmental thought toward an ill-kempt woman in a local store. As J.Z. sent a negative thought, Ramtha had her look into the woman's heart and feel the love the beleaguered single mother felt toward her children. Far from her shabby outer appearance, she had a beautiful heart.

There is a saying in the East: When the student is ready, the Master appears. How does the master know we are ready? By our thoughts. Basically, higher thoughts will reach the masters on the other side, while vile ones repel spiritual development. How often do mediums judge each other? Or worse yet, stoop to thoughts of jealousy? If you wish to advance spiritually, remember to practice positive thinking, as your master guide may be tuning in.

The Law of Thought is especially important in the séance room. Hudson Tuttle remarks in his book *Mediumship and Its Laws*: "Intense grief or anxiety shuts out the light of inspiration as clouds, the sunshine."[3] He continues, "This sadness is projected to our spirit friends who are made to bear a double grief, their own and ours."[4] It seems the spirits of the loved miss us as much as we miss them!

The Law of Continuity is essential for mediumship as it states life is continuous and there is no break between physical and spiritual laws. The fact that we survive the change called death should be viewed as positive. However, we have an obligation to remain in the body until the spiritual work is complete.

One of the tenets of Spiritualism is, "We create our own happiness or unhappiness as we obey or disobey nature's physical and Divine laws."[4] Thus, one who commits suicide is held accountable, unless mentally deranged. Oftentimes, those who are contemplating suicide, do not realize that they are taking the more difficult path. However, Spiritualism also teaches that: "We affirm that the doorway to reformation is never closed against any soul here or hereafter."[5]

When the seeker recognizes oneness with the Universe, he or she can attract greater happiness through the Law of Abundance. Few realize that we can draw abundance by aligning with the Divine mind. For instance, many spiritual practitioners reply on positive affirmations such as, "Supply is omnipresent," to create this connection. Remember, though, abundance can be many things – love, health, and happiness as well as wealth.

Sooner or later, each person receives exactly what he or she has earned through the Law of Compensation. This law covers both positive and negative actions and thoughts. When we are stubborn and refuse to grant forgiveness to our fellow man, we will suffer negative karma through this law. A Course in Miracles recommends forgiveness:

> To forgive is to overlook. Look, then, beyond error and do not
> let your perception rest upon it, for you will believe what your
> perception holds.[6]

Thus, by overlooking the faults of others, we create a more affirming atmosphere, so positive change can take place. When we judge another, we create negativity which can lead to destructive thoughts such as rivalry. Simply expressed in the text: "Forgiveness is the key to happiness."[7]

By the way, *A Course in Miracles* claims to be channeled by Jesus the Christ who taught the Law of Love: "Love one another as I have loved you." Living with a loving attitude can bring emotional freedom from hate, jealousy, and resentment. While changes such as death, illness, divorce, and debt are not pleasant, they can be mitigated by love. For instance, a trip to Egypt can be costly, but the extra work to pay the debt can be viewed as worthwhile if you enjoyed the journey or received a spiritual benefit.

Finally, the Law of Balance. Edgar Cayce, America's greatest prophet, advocated balance of body, mind, and spirit. His guides frequently reminded those seeking health and harmony: Spirit is the life, mind is the builder, and the physical is the result.[8] The Source, Cayce's guide, advised those who were ill to look within and live a more balanced life.

Rev. Andrew Jackson Davis phrased it this way: "Under all circumstances, keep an even mind."[9] As doctors explain, a lack of chemical balance in the body can lead to physical and mental illness if not addressed. Psychologists attribute separation and divorce to one-sided attitudes. Last, but not least, imbalances of power can lead to wars like the French Revolution or Civil War in the United States.

While the laws are important, so is compassion; it is the duty of the medium to guide those less fortunate and treat others with compassion. As Madame Helena Blavatsky stated a century ago:

Compassion is the Law of Laws – eternal harmony.[10]

Rev. Andrew Jackson Davis

End Notes

1. Andrew Jackson Davis, *From Fire Mist to Man*.
2. henrydrummond.wwwhubs.com/.
3. Hudson Tuttle, *Mediumship and its Laws*, National Spiritualist Association of Churches, Cassadaga, FL 1974, page 29.
4. www.nsac.org/Principles.aspx?id=3.0.
5. www.nsac.org/Principles.aspx?id=3.0.
6. www.unifying.com/forgiveness-gratitude/complete-forgiveness2.htm
7. *A Course in Miracles*, page 268.
8. www.healingcancernaturally.com/edgar-cayce-health-readings.html.
9. www.insearchofspirit.com/Spiritualism.html.
10. www.blavatsky.net/.

Suggested Reading

Rhonda Byrne. *The Secret*
Diana Cooper. *A Little Light on the Spiritual Laws*
Henry Drummond. *Natural Law in the Spiritual World*
Ralph Waldo Emerson. *Spiritual Laws*
Jerry and Ester Hicks. *The Law of Attraction*

Five

Varieties of Mental and Physical Mediumship

I myself believe that the evidence for God lies primarily in inner personal experiences.

~William James

Enlightened spirits seek compassionate people as their mediums. Once sincere seekers open their hearts, they attract the attention of master guides who will be instrumental in developing in mediumship. Chief among them will be a chemist, a doctor of philosophy, and a gatekeeper.

Mediums are then guided by spirit into various aspects of the work according to their talents. There are several types of mediumship: mental mediumship, trance, physical mediumship, and healing. However, most mediums tend to specialize in one area or another. For example, Harry Edwards was a trance medium who specialized in healing that included both mental and physical aspects of the work.

Why is mediumship so important? Several reasons come to mind: One, comfort to the bereaved; two, evidence that people survive death, and finally higher knowledge. While, master guides – Lazarus, and Ramtha to name two – come to help humanity, most spirits wish to reassure those on the earth plane that they have survived the change called death. They can also bring through helpful messages, as in the case of Mark Ireland, son of deceased psychic Richard Ireland. After Mark's son died, Mark sought the services of medium Allison DuBois. Not only did Mark contact his son, but his father, Richard Ireland who had died twelve years before. Recently, he had received his father's unpublished manuscript from a friend of his father's. In the reading, Allison Dubois gave Mark this message from his father: "I see him signing a book and handing it over to you."[1]

As you can see from this example, mediumship is a three-way process involving, spirit, medium, and sitter. Of course, not every spirit is as persistent as that of Rev. Richard Ireland, nor is every medium as gifted as Allison Dubois. However, when the right attitude is present, miracles can occur. Sometimes the sitter, though receptive, may be slow to understand the importance of the message. For instance, Mark Ireland did not immediately act on the message from his father. He needed another nudge from a psychic friend, Debra, who relayed the message: "This is a sacred book."[2] Mark Ireland finally submitted his father's book to a publisher. In 2010, *Your Psychic Potential* was published by North Atlantic Books.

While the sitter must be receptive to spirit, it is also vital that the medium maintain high ethical standards. Nothing is more draining than concern about profiting materially. It is true that "a servant is worthy of his hire," however, exorbitant fees can lower the vibration. Also, the same goes for the sitter. If a sitter only wishes to ask questions regarding property, stocks, or inherence, then the greed of the sitter can lower the energy of the séance room. By the way, when the vibrations are low, mischievous spirits can wander in. Sometimes they will even try to masquerade as famous people.

Once satisfactory conditions are established, mediums generally tune into spirit through clairaudience, clairsentience, clairgustance. In the case of mental mediumship, the medium will feel, hear, or see spirit and convey these impressions to the sitter. It is imperative that the mental medium relay messages from the other side with a minimum of distortion. Often the medium is overshadowed by spirit or in some instances is completely taken over by the spirit operator.

While the sitter has to rely on the impressions of the mental medium, the physical medium can create phenomena which is experienced through one or more of the physical human senses by all present. This is because the spirit operators manipulate, move, or transform physical energies. Examples of physical mediumship include psychokinesis, transfiguration, etherization, materialization, production of apports, precipitation, trumpet and direct voice, psychic photography, and electronic voice phenomena. While physical mediumship is much rarer than mental mediumship, when it does occur, it is very evidential.

One of the reasons that mental mediumship is more common is simply because it requires less energy and hence is less of a strain on the medium's body. In this type of mediumship, spirit creates a link between the medium and the sitter's guides. The medium then picks up the messages by utilizing the five psychic senses which correspond to the five physical senses as follows.

Types of Mental Mediumship

Clairaudience:

Psychic Hearing in which the medium hears the voices from spirit, music, or other noises from the spirit world. Often the sounds seem to come from a distance. This is because spirit may form an astral tube to amplify the sound.

Clairgustance:

Psychic smelling or tasting. A medium may taste apple pie in her mouth or smell tobacco.

Clairsentience:

Psychic feeling. The medium feels or senses the presence of spirit. Sometimes this is accompanied by a change in temperature, literally the hair on the medium's arms raises, or she may feel a chill down her back.

Clairvoyance:

Psychic seeing. A medium will see spirit either objective in front of her or with her eyes closed, so she can focus on her mind's eye.

Psychometry:

Ability to read energy by holding an object such as a watch or a ring. A medium can pick up vibrations of the past, present, and future for the owner.

Often mediums will hold an object to tune into spirit by using all these psychic senses. For example, a sensitive might hold the sitter's watch or ring to gain impression. He or she might sense the presence of a grandmother in spirit, hear her name "Catherine," then see her face or even taste her apple pie. The message would go something like this: "I sense the spirit of a grandmother here – Catherine. She looks about seventy with gray hair in a neat bun and wire-rimmed glasses. She liked to bake – apple pies were her specialty."

Not only are mediums gifted, but children can often be quite intuitive, some are even clairvoyant. A wonderful example of childhood clairvoyance is found in Cyril Scott's classic, *A Boy Who Saw True*. This diary of a sensitive boy who grows up in Victorian England detailed his ability to see auras and spirits, and converse with a guide called the Elder Brother. In consequence, he was misunderstood and often suffered as result of his gift of clairvoyance.

Clairvoyance, by the way, can take two forms – subjective and objective. Frequently, the medium receives images in the mind's eye. That is why so many clairvoyants close their eyes when they give readings, so they can focus on the inner image. Less common is the ability to see the image or spirit with the physical eye.

It may take many years of mental mediumship to develop full trance in which the spirit of the medium withdraws, and a guide steps in. The process usually begins with overshadowing, then light trance, and proceeds to full or "dead" trance. Edgar Cayce, Andrew Jackson Davis, and Elwood Babbitt were all natural trance mediums. Cayce even allowed scientists to test his trance state by removing a toe nail. When he awoke to severe pain, he decided against further experimentation.

How does trance occur? As with all phases of mediumship, it is collaborative effort between spirit and medium. Since communication from spirit in all instances passes thought the consciousness of the medium, the medium's thoughts and prejudices will influence the communication. However, the deeper the trance level of the medium, the less the consciousness of the medium is present to influence communication. This is why spirit communicators blend their energy with that of the medium in the early stages of trance, and later, with the medium's permission, take control of the medium's faculties. When in deep trance, the medium does not remember what he or she has said. The guide then is free to give personal readings, do medical diagnosis, deliver sermons, and even perform automatic writing.

One caveat before taking pen in hand: It is advisable to know the identity of the spirit control. Why? Opening the door to spirit without knowing who is on the other side is just as dangerous as opening the front door of your home to a stranger. A wayward spirit can be just as dangerous as a city thug.

In fact, Monica, a mother of four teenagers found out this danger when she tried her hand at automatic writing. This intelligent woman with a degree in English was enthralled to be communicating with a guide. However, when the guide began to take all Monica's free time, she had second thoughts. After many sleepless nights, she knew the guide had to go. With the help of a psychic friend, she ordered the spirit to leave. When she was more rested, she reviewed the channeled material, which she realized was filled with half-truths. As in all forms of mediumship, test the spirit. If the information coming though is not true, immediately stop the practice of automatic writing before a negative spirit takes over and controls your thoughts – and life!

Mediums should never tolerate irrational thought or destructive behavior. They must make an effort to develop slowly with full control of spirit. Often mediumship progresses on a continuum from mental mediumship to trance mediumship to physical phenomena. However, most mediums tend to specialize in one area or another. For example, Harry Edwards was a trance medium who specialized in healing, which includes both mental and physical aspects of mediumship.

A medium may also pray or say affirmations for those needing healing. It is also possible to utilize laying on of hands healing. When a healer places his or her hands on a patient's body, energy flows from spirit doctors and guides to the patient. The best known healing medium was the late Harry Edwards (1893-1976). He believed that healing occurred "by means of prayer; there comes a link-up with God's healing ministers in spirit who are carrying out the divine purpose of using spiritual healing as a means of awakening man's spiritual awareness."[3]

One of the most amazing aspects of spiritual healing is psychic surgery which is practiced in the Philippines by practitioners such as Alex Orbito and in Brazil by John of God who performs visible and invisible surgeries. A humble man, John of God explains: "I do not cure anybody. God heals, and in his infinite goodness permits the Entities to heal and console my brothers."

According to Heather Cumming: "When John of God channels the helping spirits they completely incorporate, taking over his body and mind. One by one, the people who visit him pass before him and are scanned by the spirit entities who perform the necessary healing."[4]

For some, the effect is felt immediately, however, for most, the healing takes place over time.

Other forms of physical mediumship include table tipping, levitation, electronic voice phenomena, psychic photography, direct voice, slate writing, materialization, apports, and precipitated painting.

Types of Physical Mediumship

Apports:
Objects that are materialized in the presence of a medium.

Direct Voice:
Spirit voices that can be heard by everyone in the séance room.

Electronic Voice Phenomena: (EVP):
Spirit voices and intelligent sounds produced by electronic devices.

Materialization:
Appearance of spirit via formation of ectoplasm from a medium.

Precipitated Paintings:

Pictures which have been formed or precipitated by spirit artists.

Psychic Photography:

The ability to capture the image of spirit on film.

Psychokinesis:

Movement of objects/people without any physical means of support.

Slate Writing:

The practice of spirit writing messages on slates.

Table Tipping:

Communicating from spirit by means of spirit raps on a table.

Transfiguration:

A mask of ectoplasm covering a medium's features so that the face of spirit appears.

One of the most dramatic forms of physical mediumship, levitation, has been documented by the Catholic Church. St. Ignatius of Loyola had this gift, as well as Spiritualist medium, Daniel Douglas Home, who was often ridiculed by Christian churches. Home (1833–1886) lived during the heyday of Spiritualism when many forms of physical mediumship were practiced.

One of the most fascinating examples of physical mediumship was slate writing. Victorian Spiritualist would place two clean slates together with a piece of chalk was between the slates. While the phenomena could occur in daylight, most mediums preferred the slates to be in darkness. Often they would place the sealed slates in a light proof box which was placed in the center of the séance table. Then the physical medium who usually sat at the head of the table went into trance, while the group meditated. Within moments, the sound of chalk scratching across the slates was heard by all present. When the sealed slates were opened, messages, sometimes in several languages, or even pictures were on the slates. According to Ron Nagy, author of *Slate Writing: Invisible Intelligences,* as many as thirty-three different colors were produced on one slate – with just one piece of white chalk placed between the two slates. Also, spirits such as President Abraham Lincoln, signed their names!

While Victorian spirits used children's slates to convey their messages from the other side, twentieth-century spirits of the departed may choose to place their messages on tape or film. The medium, Leslie Flint, (1911-1994) brought through voices of the dead which could be heard by their friends or relatives. While some of the voices were in a whisper, that of Mahatma Gandhi came through with clarity. The famous philosopher brought through this message:

> The first lesson one must learn is to forget oneself, to give out in love all that is possible from within yourself, and it shall be returned to you. These things that Christ spoke about, and all the great teachers, all the great philosophers down through the ages was that man should forget himself, so that in return he might find himself.

Ghost hunters and researchers also use tape recorders to capture voices of spirit at haunted sites. In 1993, two British couples tried their hand at EVP with some remarkable results. Robin and Sandy Foy and Diane and Alan Bennett contacted a guide named Manu whose voice came through on their tape recorder, as well as an audible performance of Rachmaninoff's Second Concerto.

The group chronicled their physical phenomena in a book entitled, *The Scole Experiment*. Recently, medium Brian Hurst invited the four to the United States for a series of séances which included direct voice in which everyone heard or experienced spirit, levitation, touches, lights, and an opportunity to ask spirit questions. James Van Praagh asked about the spiritual level from which the guides originated. Edwin, a philosopher speaking through Alan informed James that the spirit controls had to be highly evolved in order to manipulate the energies of the universe and be of service to Mankind.[6]

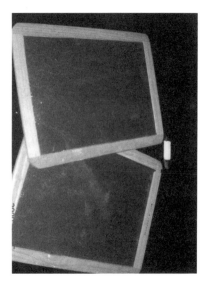

Children's slates used by Spiritualists for slate writing

The Scole Group which continued for five years was also known for its psychic photography. While it is not uncommon for photographers to capture spirit in the form of orbs in photograph, few receive such "handwriting, symbols, and messages which appear on factory-sealed, unopened photographic film, and objects, lights, and solid beings which materialized before previously skeptical observers."[7]

Materialization is perhaps the most controversial aspect of physical mediumship. It can take several forms – transfiguration, etherization, apports, and precipitated painting. Spirit will transfigure over a medium's face in the beginning. Later, when more ectoplasm is formed, partial materialization occurs. In rare instances, full materializations occur such as those of the medium, Eva Carrière, which were photographed in red light by Charles Richet. Later, Ethel Post Parrish produced amazing materialization at Camp Silver Belle in Pennsylvania. Those who attended her séances claim the materialization of Mrs. Parrish's guide, Silver Belle, was so clear you could see the spirit's eye lashes!

End Notes

1. Richard Ireland, *Your Psychic Potential*, North Atlantic Books, Berkeley, CA 2010, page xvi.
2. Richard Ireland, *Your Psychic Potential*, North Atlantic Books, Berkeley, CA 2010, page xvii.
3. http://www.usa-psychics.com/harry-edwards.html.
4. http://www.healingquests.com.
5. http://www.LeslieFlint.com.
6. www.afterlife101.com/Scole_1.html.
7. Brian Hurst, *Heaven Can Help*, iUniverse, Lincoln Ne, 2007, page 209.

Suggested Reading

Peggy Barns. *Lo I Am With You Always*
Arthur Hasting. *On the Tongues of Angels*
Brian Hurst. *Heaven Can Help*
Richard Ireland. *Your Psychic Potential*
Elaine Kuzmeskus. *Séance 101*
Sidney Kirkpatrick. *Edgar Cayce: An American Prophet*
Jess Stearn. *The Sleeping Prophet*
James Van Praagh. *Heaven and Earth*

Six

Dream Visitations

In sleep we enter upon the same life as that we enter between death and birth.

~W.B. Yeats

As Dr. Sigmund Freud pointed out a century ago:

Dreams are the royal road to the unconscious mind.

They are also the royal road to the super conscious mind. With a little practice, dreams supply easy access to psychic information as well as a safe way to contact the other side. This is because we are all psychic in the dream – a fact well understood by ancient cultures.

The ancient Egyptians, Greeks, Hindus, and the Tibetans all knew that the veil between the two worlds is lifted during sleep. According to E.A. Wallis Budge, translator of *The Egyptian Book of the Dead*, the Egyptians believed that "Ka," the astral body, and "Ba," the soul, could leave the physical body at will. They believed this "Ka" or akashic energy was connected to the physical body by cord of "silvery light." In order to insure a safe passage to the other side, *The Egyptian Book of the Dead* lists prayers and incantations for the safe passage of the soul.

With their firm belief in an afterlife, the ancient Egyptians viewed dreams as a distinct place. According to dream expert, Robert Moss:

If you were an Egyptian, you did not "have" a dream you saw or experienced something inside a dream, which was a place.[1]

Dreams then become a real location to explore. The ancients believed we made this journey to the other side on a boat:

The Egyptians hoped they might be permitted to travel on the boat of Ra across the primeval waters of Nun – the substance of the Dwat or underworld – through all the stages of testing, recollection, life review to a glorious rebirth.[2]

The Greeks, undoubtedly influenced by the Egyptians saw dreams as a valid method of healing. They even dedicated their healing temples to the God of Healing, Asclepius. Those in need of healing were encouraged to sleep in the temple overnight in the hope that the Asclepius would appear in a dream. According to dream researcher, Ed Tick, the process would take hours or days:

> Upon entering the abaton, the seeker was put in a narrow womb-like chamber. There the seeker waited for hours or days for a healing vision or dream in which Asclepius in one of his guises – god, bearded man, boy, snake, or dog – appeared.[3]

Skilled dream analysts would later interpret the healing dreams.

Dreams in which we receive visitations from guides such Asclepius are called lucid dreams – a term coined by Dr. Stephen Leberge. In these vivid dreams, the dreamer is consciously aware that he or she is dreaming. Frequently, this type of dream will contain information that goes beyond the person's consciousness ability:

> The *Vigyan Bhairav Tantra* is another ancient Hindu tract that describes how best to direct consciousness within the dream and vision states of sleep. The Tibetans also use dreams to contact the dead and to diagnose illnesses.[4]

In *The Tibetan Book of the Dead*, they describe lucid dream states, spiritual practices, and the relationship between life and death. Also Tibetans of the Bon sect have particular faith in dreams:

> Tibetan Bon faith healers used dreams to read the relationship between the spirits and humans, and diagnose diseases. "Dream tellers" were also involved with the government to make predictions to the kings about the politics and prosperity of the country.[5]

Finally, the Tibetan text on dreams, *The Dawning of the Clear Light*, advised surrender to the Divine as a means to inner illumination.

This inner illumination found in dreams has inspired scientists and writers. For example, physicist Niels Bohr gained insight into the structure of the atom from a dream:

> One night he dreamed of a sun composed of burning gases, with planets orbiting it, attached by fine threads. When he

awoke, he realized it was the solution to his puzzle. It explained the structure of the atom and heralded the birth of atomic physics.[6]

Many writers have also been inspired by dreams, chief among them Charles Dickens, Graham Greene, Jack Kerouac, and Jules Verne. Dickens was known to receive plots, characters, and even names of characters in dreams, while Jack Kerouac's dreams inspired novels, *On the Road*, *The Dharma Bums*, and a whole book on dreams, *The Book of Dreams*.

Mark Twain not only received material in dreams but also met dead relatives and friends. He even foresaw his own brother's accidental death. In his notebook he described conversation with "the living and dead, rational and irrational." Twain was one of many who report talking to their deceased relatives in dreams. How is this possible? While the physical body is fast asleep, the sleeper can travel in his astral body to visit discarnates who dwell in the astral plane and beyond. Often loved ones and guides will descend to the astral plane to aid in communication. However, it is wise not to force such contact. Dr. Harmon Bro in *Edgar Cayce on Dreams* commented on spirit contact:

> Cayce confirmed that this (the dream) had been authentic contact, and warned again, as he had already told the dream, that to seek contact too often with a discarnate would bring distress to the discarnate, holding them back from their own full journey.[7]

Astral travel is another phenomena reported in dreams. Oliver Fox had many out-of-body experiences which he chronicled in his book *Astral Projection*. These states provided rare glimpses into the other side:

> Instantly the vividness of life increased a hundred fold. Never had the sea, sky, and trees shone with such glamorous beauty; even the commonplace houses seem alive and especially beautiful. Never had I felt so absurdly well, so clear brained, so inexpressively free! The sensation was exquisite beyond words, but it lasted only a few minutes and I awoke.[8]

A. E. Powell, an English theosophist, also described astral travel. He felt the function of the astral body was "to make sensation possible, to serve as a bridge between the mind and the physical body, and to act as an independent vehicle of consciousness.[9] It is in the dream state that the astral body functions independent of the physical. Powell believed that there was a great spiritual benefit in dreams and astral travel. Conversely, with mental growth the quality of dreams could be improved. Every impulse sent by the mind to the physical brain has to pass through the astral body, and as astral matter is far more responsive to thought vibrations than is physical matter, it follows that the effects produced on the astral body are correspondingly greater – thus when a man has acquired mental control, i.e., has learned to dominate the brain, to concentrate, to think. As he does so, a corresponding change will take place in his astral life; and if he brings the memory of that life through into the physical brain, his dreams will become vivid, well-sustained, rational and even instructive.[10] Powell further explained how, during sleep, the spiritual seeker may contact "Invisible Helpers." He also believed "mediums and psychics project their astral bodies unconsciously when they go into trance, but usually, on coming out of trance, there is no brain memory of the experience acquired.[11]

Keeping a dream journal then is an important step to developing mediumship. If you wish to use this method, here are some suggestions if you wish to "catch" a dream:

1. Before going to bed, place a notebook (a nice thick one) on your night stand. Give yourself the suggestion, "I will remember my dreams in every detail."
2. When you awake, write something in your dream journal, even if it is only a fragment or feeling.
3. If you are unable to remember a dream, try setting the alarm clock for the middle of your sleep cycle when you are more likely to hit Rapid Eye Movement or dream sleep.
4. Another suggestion to induce dreaming is to wake up fully, then go back to bed for awhile. Often you will drift into the light stage one sleep of dreams and you will remember a dream when you awaken from your second sleep.
5. Once you have recorded the dream, save it for later in the day for more careful study. When you have more time, make a permanent record of your dreams in a journal.

Once you have remembered your dream, it is important to interpret it properly. First decide on which level you are dreaming—physical, mental/emotional, or spiritual. Many a dreamer feels like he is in a typhoon as a result of churning stomach or he is surrounded by sirens as he incorporates the morning "alarm" into the dream. These purely physical dreams are less common. The most common type of dream is the mental/emotional ones in which the dreamer tries to fathom his life. Often these dreams give insight into life's problems and aid in decision-making. More vivid dreams in which you know you are dreaming are termed lucid dreams. Frequently, there is an authority figure present to guide the dreamer. These lucid dreams are spiritual gifts of inspiration.

Study spiritual dreams carefully, as they preview the future. Medical intuitive Winter Robinson realized this to be true when she had a lucid dream after separating from her first husband, leaving her job, and moving to Rhode Island:

> A few months later, I awoke in the middle of the night to a clear
> voice that said, "Waiting for Michael."[12]

Within the year, she met her future husband, Michael, at the Monroe Institute in Virginia.

After the level is determined, work on interpreting the symbols present in the dream. Symbols may be either personal or universal in nature. For example, if your grandfather, Harry, chewed Edgewood Tobacco, then a blue metal Edgewood Pipe Tobacco canister would represent your grandfather. Similarly, if you Aunt Catherine loved lilacs, then lilacs would be a personal symbol for Aunt Catherine.

On the other hand, the dreamer may see a tree, which is universal symbol for the tree of life. Or a ladder may represent the ladder of success. A house, for example, may have many symbols within its walls. The porch may represent the outer façade. The living room would be symbolic of social life and may indicate the state of friendships. The bedroom would be indicative of a marriage or more intimate relationships. The basement represents the subconscious mind, while the attic is the higher mind. Even our bodies are symbolic. The eyes are the "windows of the soul," the hands represent work, and the feet, humility or grounding. Blood is the connection to "blood relatives" and the bones are the foundation of the body.

Colors also have their own association. The natural color spectrum goes from infrared to ultraviolet. Red, the first color, represents the raw energy of life – physical strength, and sex. It can also show a temper! Orange, a sacred color in the East, is an out-going color in the West. Orange shows pride, vitality, and health. Clairvoyantly, some orange in the aura draws attention and can improve finances! However, too much orange can be overbearing. Yellow is the color of sunshine and as such shows a positive mental attitude and a clever mind. Pale yellow, though, can be timid. Green, the middle color of the spectrum, indicates harmony and health. Edgar Cayce said "green with a dash of blue" is excellent for healing. Blue is the heavenly color, representing spiritual qualities. Aqua is seen in the aura of an idealist who wishes to help others in a practical way. True blue is even purer in intentions, with cobalt blue indicting the deepest and most psychic qualities. However, if the shade of blue is too dark, depression may be present. Purple, the last color of the spectrum may indicate change, according to Edgar Cayce. Once the decision is made, the purple settles into blue. Purple is also the color of royalty and often designates one with a devotional nature and deep sincerity.

Numbers are also highly significant in dreams. For instance, Dr. Bernie Siegel, author of *Man, Medicine, and Miracles*, often asked his patients to draw a picture of the their illness and a second picture depicting how they saw themselves getting well. The doctor paid close attention to numbers in these drawings. One woman who had only seven months to live, drew seven flowers in front of her house.

Numbers also have universal meanings. For example, the number one indicates uniqueness, standing alone. It shows the spirit of the pioneer. Two is a relationship number as it is the number of the couple or marriage. Two indicates attraction. Three is the number of manifestation – man, woman, and child. It is an excellent number for communication. Four indicates stability and the slow success of the square. It is the number of building. Five, the number of the pentacle, is magical. This lucky number indicates adventure and success in undertakings. Six, on the other hand, indicates service and domestic qualities. It is the number of harmony. Seven is considered to be the perfect individual number, and as such it is mystical and very spiritual. Eight, a double four, can indicate great strength, but also great obstacles. Eight shows success after hard work. Nine is considered the luckiest number in the East as it is the number of the guru. In the West nine indicates travel and adventure. It is the number of the free spirit. Ten becomes a one, while eleven since it is a double digit is considered a master number like twenty-two and thirty-three. Twelve is considered to be the best number for groups – hence the twelve apostles!

In conclusion, dreams can be a direct route to the super-conscious mind. If you have a question you wish to pose to the Universal Mind or wish to contact a loved one or guide on the other side, write your request on a slip of paper. Be specific. Then for the next three nights, sleep with the slip of paper under your pillow. Expect an answer in a dream. If you do not receive one, try rewording the question and give the matter a second try. With practice, dreams can provide visitations with the so-called dead as well as provide answers – if you are open to spirit.

Dream Symbols

Following are charts advising meanings of various dream parts.

Colors

Red	Vital physical energy, sex, anger, in debt, stop
Orange	Pride, courage, sacred color in the East
Yellow	Sunshine, cheerfulness, mental color
Green	Harmony, health, patience
Blue	Sky, spiritual color, "blue" or sad mood
Purple	Royalty, unique, older person
White	Purity, medical field, spiritual, positive
Black	Void, negative
Gray	Unsure, worry
Brown	Earth, materialistic

Numbers

One	Stands alone, unique, pioneer
Two	A couple, pair
Three	Manifestation, the trinity
Four	Four-square, secure, obstacles
Five	Pentacle, magic, creativity
Six	Service
Seven	Spiritual number, best individual number
Eight	Two fours, obstacles, security that is earned
Nine	Travel, adventure
Ten	Interpret as one
Eleven	Double number stays the same, lucky for goals
Twelve	Spiritual number, best number for a group
Thirteen	Twelve plus one, an occult number, at times unlucky number

Gems and Metals

Amethyst	Saint Germain, psychic energy, spiritual healing
Diamond	Lucky, purity, leadership "king of gems"
Emerald	Healing, peace, prosperity, eyesight
Gold	King of metals, relates to God, attainment, the Sun, and leadership
Jade	Orient, improves life force
Lapis	Egypt, enhances spiritual and psychic force
Pearl	Feminine, purity, improves fertility
Sapphire	Spiritual, high minded, lifts depression
Silver	Queen of metals, relates to Goddess, knowledge, Moon and fertility
Ruby	Highest earthly attainment, riches, gives energy
Rose Quartz	Love, heart center, improves circulation
Turquoise	American Indian, tranquility

Animals

Bee	Industry
Bear	Protection
Bugs	Problems, irritation
Butterfly	Transformation, reincarnation
Cat	Egyptian, psychic, or "catty"-critical
Dog	Faithful, loyal, friendly
Eagle	Vision, high spirituality, legal profession
Humming Bird	Messenger between the two worlds, happiness
Giraffe	Higher perspective, gentle
Monkey	Immature, funny
Lady Bug	Good luck
Peacock	Clairvoyance
Snake	Change, evil, sexual, gossip, wisdom, kundalini

Common Symbols

Air	Communication
Baby	New beginning
Badge	Authority
Book	Knowledge, study
Boulder	Obstacle
Bridge	Transition, relationship
Cake	Birthday, celebration
Car	Transportation, dreamer
Cave	Private place, meditation
Circle	Unity, group
Clock	Time
Coins	Money, prosperity
Daisy	Making a decision
Death	An ending
Door	Opportunity
Fire	Spirit, anger
Flag	Military Service
Harp	Music, harmony, Ireland
Ladder	Achievement
Moon	Psychic, mystical, feminine
Music	Harmony, rainbow, psychic
Rose	Love
Sand	Shifts
Sun	Recognition, attainment, masculine
Shopping	Decision making
Pen	Writing
Telephone	Communication
Water	Emotions
Woods	Confusion

Face

Hair	Thinking
Eyes	Window of the soul
Ears	Listening, communication
Lips	Speech
Teeth	Speech

House

Front door	Facade
Back door	Secret
Living room	Social life
Bedroom	Marriage, sleep, or sex
Kitchen	Food, nutrition
Dining Room	Social, family gathering
Bathroom	Cleansing
Basement	Foundation
Attic	Higher Mind

End Notes

1. Robert Moss, *The Dreamers Book of the Dead*, Destiny Books, Rochester, NY, 2005, page 92.
2. Robert Moss, *The Dreamers Book of the Dead*, Destiny Books, Rochester, NY, 2005, page 214.
3. Ed Tick, *The Practice of Dream Healing*, 2008, Quest Books, Wheaton IL, page 5.
4. www.dreamtree.com/inside/tag/tibetan-book-of-the-dead/.
5. www.tibetanmedicine-edu.org/index.php dream-practice.
6. Craig and Jane Parker-Hamilton, *The Psychic Workbook*, Vermillon Press, London, page 159.
7. Harmon Hartzel Bro, *Edgar Cayce on Dreams*, Warner Books, page 81.
8. Oliver Fox, *Astral Projection*, University Books, New Hyde Park NY, 1962, pages 32-33.

9. E. Powell, *The Astral Body*, The Theosophical Publishing House, Wheaton, IL, 1927, page 23.
10. A. E. Powell, *The Astral Body*, The Theosophical Publishing House, Wheaton, IL, 1927, page 95.
11. E. Powell, *The Astral Body*, The Theosophical Publishing House, Wheaton, IL, 1927, page 106.
12. Winter Robinson, *A Hidden Order*, Red Wheel Press, York Beach, ME, page 12.

Suggested Reading

Harmon Hartzel Bro. *Edgar Cayce on Dreams*
Robert Moss. *The Dreamers Book of the Dead*
Oliver Fox. *Astral Projection*
Craig Hamilton-Parker. *Remembering Your Dreams*
Stephen Leberge. *Exploring the Lucid Power of Dreams*
A. E. Powell. *The Astral Body*
Elsie Sechrist. *Dreams: Your Magic Mirror*
Ed Tick. *The Practice of Dream Healing*
Kevin J. Todeschi. *Dream Images and Symbols*

Seven

Mediation
Portal to the Other Side

Work for God, love God alone, and be wise with God. When an ordinary man puts the necessary time and enthusiasm into meditation and prayer, he becomes a divine man.

~Paramahansa Yogananda

Meditation is the most common method of contacting the other side after dreams. It may take more time and effort, but the rewards are many. Basically, mediation is a stress-buster. Dr. Herbert Benson, author of *the Relaxation Response*, found that meditation was effective in lowering blood pressure and can relieving many psychosomatic ailments. More and more psychologists today are advocating "mindfulness," a form of meditation introduced by Dr. Jon Kabat-Zinn in the 1970s to reduce stress and lower anxiety.

While meditation is not only mentally helpful, it is also spiritually of benefit. We are, after all, body, mind, and spirit. In fact, clairvoyants such as C. W. Leadbeater would say we have seven bodies, each with its unique properties. Understanding the seven bodies gives a good foundation for

Elsie Sechrist and Edgar Cayce. Sechrist is author of *Dreams: Your Magic Mirror* with Edgar Cayce, *Courtesy of the Association for Research and Enlightenment.*

mediation. To begin with, each person is made up of seven bodies—physical, etheric, astral, lower mental, higher mental, spiritual, and cosmic consciousness. At the base of the spine, this spiritual energy is described as a coiled serpent in the East. When this energy called kundalini is raised through the center or chakras of the body, an ordinary person experiences creativity, intuition, and even cosmic consciousness. See the following chart.

Seven Bodies

Physical Body	Three dimensional body visible to the naked eye.
Etheric double	Exact duplicate of the physical body made of finer material. This body remains in place as a pattern for the physical, even if parts of the physical are amputated.
Astral or emotional body	Fine energy body which can detach during the sleep state for astral travel.
Mental body	This body works with consciousness. When developed, can bring in synchronicity and telepathy.
Higher mental body or manas	Finer than the lower, mechanical mind, is associated with philosophy and world of creation.
Soul or Buddhic body	Individual portion of God. This body when fully active, opens the mystical third eye and is responsible for clairvoyance.
God or Atma	Cosmic consciousness or full realization of all that is.

In addition to the seven bodies, there are seven major energy centers or chakras. C.W. Leadbeater, who wrote the definitive book on the chakras, used his clairvoyance to view each one. Leadbeater's clairvoyance was so remarkable that he was able to peer inside an atom before microscopes were invented that were powerful enough to penetrate the atom's microscopic structure. When microscopes were invented, scientists saw the same structures Leadbeater had described many years before in *Occult Chemistry*.

According to Leadbeater, the chakras are circular in nature with spokes of energy radiating from the center. The chakras increase in number of spokes, radiation, and intensity, as they advance up the spine. For example, the first chakra, the root chakra, has only four spokes; while the top or seventh center is referred to as "the lotus of a thousand petals." The chakras also vary in color from infra-red to ultra-violet.

First Chakra

To begin, the first chakra, the root chakra, is at the base of the spine, has four petals and is associated with the color red and the adrenal glands. When this chakra is out of balance, a person feels unsupported by the universe. Positive attributes include feeling grounded and secure.

Second Chakra

The second chakra has six petals and is located over the spleen. It vibrates to the color orange and is associated with sex and glamour. It governs the pancreas, diseases of the pancreas, and also the spleen and intestines. In the East, intestines are associated with memory. When the second chakra is opened, glamour and worldly success manifest.

Third Chakra

The third chakra which contains ten petals, is located on in the area of the solar plexus. This chakra is associated with personal power and ego, and governs the adrenal glands. When the third chakra is opened wide, a well-developed intellect, leadership, and confidence are evident. When there is dysfunction, stomach problems, especially ulcers may manifest. No wonder ulcers are often called "the executive disease."

Fourth Chakra

The fourth chakra is located at the heart and is associated with the middle color of the spectrum, green. It has twelve petals, governs the thymus gland, and rules personal love and compassion. When this center is depressed, disorders of the immune system, such as cancer may manifest as well as heart problems. Damage to the heart center catches the victim's attention like no other center. Ram Das described his heart attack as the "last overload protection."

The last three chakras have psychic potentials: the fifth clairaudience, the sixth, clairvoyance, and the seventh, cosmic consciousness. Hence, the spokes of each successive chakra increase in velocity and number—jumping from the sixteen of the throat center to ninety-six in the sixth chakra.

Fifth Chakra

The fifth chakra is located in the throat and has sixteen petals. It governs the thyroid and its color is turquoise-blue. Imbalances in this chakra can cause speech and throat problems. Conversely, positive attributes include clarity in thought and speech, and even clairaudience.

Sixth Chakra

The sixth chakra is located in the middle of the forehead. This chakra, indigo blue in color, is associated with the pineal gland, and is sensitive to light. When blocked, depression, eye problems, and headaches may manifest. Positive attributes include vision, spiritual faith, and clairvoyance.

Seventh Chakra

The seventh chakra, the crown chakra, has nine hundred and sixty petals and governs the master gland of the body, the pituitary gland. It is known in the East as "the lotus of a thousand petals." It is a center of radiant energy. However, a soul may experience dysfunction and remain trapped emotionally between the two worlds. When this occurs, the person may have serious diseases psychoses or even remain in a coma state. However, when this chakra is opened in a positive manner, the aspirant attains self liberation, and freedom from rebirth.

Diagram of Chakras

Chakra	Place	Gland	Color	Function	Dysfunction
one	base of the spine	adrenal	red	life force	greed
two	beneath the navel	sex	orange	procreation	self gratification
three	above the navel	pancreas	yellow	power	anger
four	center of chest	thymus	green	love	depression
five	center of throat	thyroid	aqua	truth	free of expression
six	center of forehead	pineal	deep blue	vision	confusion
seven	top of the head	pituitary	purple	God	delusion

As we progress in life, the lower issues of security, sexuality, and power or ego have to be managed. Once these are in check, the seeker may begin to open the heart through love of another person (fourth Chakra). Christ and Buddha are examples of supreme love and as such were self realized with all chakras open. While the average person may only have some psychic energy, such as clairsentience, the third chakra inspiration is from the fourth or heart center. When the fifth chakra is fully activated, clairaudience may be experienced. With the sixth, clairvoyance occurs and when the seventh chakra is fully functioning, cosmic consciousness is present.

This is why psychic perception begins in the gut with clairsentience. Only gradually does it evolve to the personal inspiration that creates art, music, and poetry. Eventually, as one evolves, personal love is transformed into spiritual love, (fifth) through service to others. Then a few souls reach the level of the sixth chakra, which opens the third eye of psychic vision, while fewer still can attain cosmic consciousness of masters. Those who had opened the seventh chakra receive self realization which Eastern philosophers view as the ultimate goal of meditation.

Mediums can benefit from a study of esoteric anatomy. However, even without this knowledge, meditation is an important spiritual practice. Edgar Cayce was clear on this point:

> It is not musing, not daydreaming; but as ye find your bodies
> made up of the physical , mental and spiritual, it is the attuning
> of the mental body and the physical body to its spiritual source.[1]
> Cayce Reading 281-41 1.

Cayce suggested that the meditator practice meditation at the same time and place each day. He also advised meditators lie or sit with their backs straight, so the psychic energy could travel directly up the body. During the actual process of meditation, the life force, or kundalini, travels up the spine from the base to the upper chakras of the throat, brow, and crown which link with the thyroid, pineal, and pituitary glands.

There are many methods of meditation – both for individuals and groups. Perhaps the most advanced mediators are the Tibetan Buddhists. They advocate the Triple Gem: Buddha, Dharma, and Sangha (spiritual community). In other words, faith in God, doing one's duty, and maintaining spiritual community. Citing laziness as an obstacle to meditation, young monks are encouraged to pursue meditation with regular enthusiastic practice. After all, Tibetan Buddhists have a lofty goal – the liberation of all sentient beings.

Instructions for Meditation

1. Set aside a regular time for meditation. It is best to start with five minutes and work your way up to a twenty to thirty minute period.
2. Begin with a prayer and surround yourself with white light.
3. You may wish to lie or sit on a cushion or mat used only for that purpose, as the yogis use a meditation cushion or rug to buffer themselves against unwanted earthly influences.
4. Sit or lie down without a pillow, so that your spine is straight.
5. Then focus on soft music such as Tibetan Bowls, The Eternal Om, or Silk Road.
6. Allow your body to relax. Each time your mind wanders, attend to the music.

Eventually, you will enter a light trance state as the body relaxes. With regular practice, the meditator shifts from the waking state with Beta brain waves to the Alpha brain wave state to deep trance, indicated by Theta brain waves.

What actually happens in meditation? As the physical body becomes peaceful, the astral body can loosen from the physical body. Once the astral body is detached, the mediator can visit higher realms to make contact with loved ones, guides, and angels. With sincere effort, the meditator is welcomed to the higher planes. First the higher mental plane, the Buddhic plane, and finally Nirvana. Often there is an inner feeling of clarity, sometimes accompanied by visual or auditory sensations – perhaps seeing vivid colors or hearing spiritual music. Often, the aspirant will be in contact with loved ones or even spiritual guides. With practice, meditation can be a reliable form of contacting the other side. The practice of meditation promotes inner harmony, strengthens the aura, and creates a portal to the other side. Over a period of regular practice, meditation can help develop the gifts of telepathy, clairvoyance, and mediumship. With regular practice, the meditator will begin to open his or her third eye. An excellent way to open the psychic eye is through the yogic practice of candle meditation.

Candle Meditation

1. Say a prayer of protection such as "The Lord's Prayer" and call on your guides. If you do not know their names, call on Infinite Intelligence.
2. Then sit in a chair in a comfortable position with feet on the floor.

"Gathering the Light," Taoist meditation from *The Secret of the Golden Flower.*

3.   Place a candle on a table opposite you at eye level, about twelve to eighteen inches away. If you have long hair, you may wish to tie it back, or place the candle an arm's length.

4.   Light the candle and gaze steadily into the flames for 20 seconds or so.

5.   Then close your eyes and allow your mind's eye to follow the after image. Try to hold the image in your third eye as long as you can. If the image moves away from you gaze, concentrate on bringing it back and holding it steady. Allow your consciousness to remain steady, focusing on the image of the flame.

Try the exercise three times at first. For maximum benefit, practice this exercise at the same time and place each day. Gradually lengthen your meditation time from five to twenty minutes, as you become more comfortable. Many students report seeing a sea of faces. This is because they have crossed a portal to the other side. Do not linger on the astral plane, allow your consciousness to travel to the higher mental planes. If you practice the exercise faithfully for ninety days, you should be able to contact your loved ones and spirit guides.

End Notes

1. http://www.edgarcayce.org/spirituality/ec_on_meditation.html

Suggested Reading

Dr. Herbert Benson. *The Relaxation Response*
Dr. Deepak Chopra. *Ageless Body, Timeless Mind*
Prema Chodron. *When Things Fall Apart*
Krishan Das. *Chance of a Lifetime*
Dr. Robert Ellwood. *Quieting the Mind*
Judy Hall. *The Art of Psychic Protection*
B.K.S. Iyengar. *Light on Yoga*
Jon Kabat-Zinn. *Wherever You Go, There You Are*
Howard Murphet. *Sai Baba: Man of Miracles*
Meredith Ann Puryear. *Healing Through Meditation and Prayer*
Henry Reed. *Your Mind: Unlocking Your Hidden Powers*
Dr. Samuel Sagan. *Entity Possession*
Elsie Sechrist. *Meditation: Gateway to Light*
Baird T. Spaulding. *Life and Teachings of the Masters of the Far East*
Kevin Todeschi. *Edgar Cayce on the Akashic Records*
Paramahansa Yogananda. *Autobiography of a Yogi*

Eight

Spirit Guides

All the phenomena of mediumship are due to the operation of spirit power.

~Silver Birch

Meditation not only opens the third eye, but also may reveal the presence of spiritual guides. Some of these guides, such as personal guides, are with us at birth and stay throughout the lifespan, while others come in on a temporary basis. For instance, many writers, painters, and musicians attract spiritual helpers to assist with their creative endeavors. When their services are no longer needed, these invisible helpers depart.

Whatever their purpose, guides come when the medium is ready. American psychic, Edgar Cayce, contacted his guide in trance. In his youth, Cayce had lost his voice and consulted a local hypnotist, Al Layne, to help him regain his voice. Not only did the hypnotist restore Cayce's speech, but also he made contact with Cayce's guide known as "the Source." It wasn't long before Edgar Cayce became known as "the Sleeping Prophet."

J.Z. Knight, on the other hand, was very much present when her guide, Ramtha, stepped into her life in 1977. Her interest in backpacking led her to explore the possibility of using a replica of the Great Pyramid of Giza to preserve food for hiking trips. When she had placed a replica of the Great Pyramid on her head in jest, she saw standing in front of her the tall form of Ramtha, a 35,000-year-old warrior from Lemuria.

Sylvia Browne was just as surprised when she first saw her guide when she was eight. "Francine," the name Sylvia gave her guide, reassured her. "Don't be afraid, Sylvia; I come from God." Sylvia, however, waited until adulthood to start a professional career as a psychic on May 8, 1973, when she held a small psychic group in her home. Since then Browne has gone unto spectacular success as both a medium and an author.

While many mediums see their guides when in their childhood, others connect when they are under stress. Even though Rosemary Browne had seen spirit as a child, she did not pay much attention until she began to sit at the piano, home bound from a car accident. With little formal piano training, she found herself playing quite expertly. She believed that the spirit of Franz Liszt was guiding her hands. In her biography, *Unfinished Symphonies*, she explains that she had seen the spirit of Liszt as a child, but was not ready to take mediumship until an adult.

Mediums, by the way, usually attract several guides – a master teacher, a chemist, a personal guide, a joy guide, and an American Indian for protection.

See the following descriptions.

Spirit Guides

Personal guide	This guide is assigned before you were born and stays with you.
Master philosopher	A guide who instructs medium on philosophy and higher knowledge.
Master chemist	A guide who adjusts the chemistry of the medium's body, usually a doctor.
Joy guide	Light-hearted guide who lifts the spirits and acts as gate keepers.
American Indian	This guide acts as a protector.

Andrew Jackson Davis had the spirit of the ancient physician Galen as his doctor-teacher. While Davis never knew Galen, Arthur Ford's guide, Fletcher, was a childhood friend. Guides are also attracted by our intent. For example, John of God whose sole focus is healing, attracts many deceased physicians as guides such as Dr. Oswaldo Cruz, Dr. Augusto de Almeida, and Dr. Jose Valdivino. It is interesting to note that many mediums attract American Indian guides. For instance, English medium Estelle Robert had guides Red Cloud and Maurice Barbanell, (1902-1981). Another English medium channeled Silver Birch, an American Indian. Typical of Silver Birch's guidance was the guides' response to a question about death:

> Similarly there is weeping when people die in your world, but there is rejoicing in ours. Death means that the life has served its purpose, or should have done, and the individual is ready to enjoy all the tremendous richness and beauty that the spirit life has to offer.[2]

With such wonderful American Indian guides helping mediums, one can't help but wonder why do so many of these guides assist mediums here and abroad? It is because the American Indians were far from savage. They knew a great deal about spirit which they termed "the great spirit" and the spirit world which they called "the happy hunting grounds." They were also experts in prophecy and Shamanic medicine. When they were cruelly slaughtered by the white man, many chose to remain on the other side, rather than reincarnate. Often they willingly take on the spiritual duty as protector for those who wish to walk between the two worlds. According to Frederick Harding:

> The Indians, as Spirit Guides, must keep away and out of the medium's aura and range of instrumentality mischievous entities which are attracted by the operating line of manifestations.[3]

In other words, the energy of mediums may attract good and negative spirits. It is the job of the Redman to repel the mischievous spirits either singly or in bands on the other side.

Everyone has guides, but not everyone knows who they are. With practice, students can tune into their guides through dreams. Once you become more adept at dreaming, you can control your lucid dream state. Send the thought that you would like to meet your guide face to face. Then make the effort to go to bed an hour early and allow ample time to record your dream in the morning.

The same is true of meditation. It is possible to witness guides – even receive the names of your guides and messages in meditation. Try the "Meet Your Guide Meditation" at the end of the chapter to contact your spirit guide through meditation. Of course, a seeker can always consult a medium to find out more about guides.

Mediums tune into spirit guides with clairsentience/ psychic feeling, clairaudience/psychic hearing, and clairvoyance/psychic seeing. When James Van Praagh saw clairvoyant Irene Martin-Giles, she was told he had a nun – Sister Theresa– as his guide.

> The clairvoyant described Sister Theresa in detail, right down to the brilliant blue color of her eyes.[1]

The medium also told Van Praagh that he had a Chinese spiritual teacher, Chang.

Spirit artists can actually draw a picture of your guide. The author witnessed this in Camp Chesterfield when spirit artist Rev. Phyllis Kennedy created a portrait of her Tibetan guide. Other fine psychic artists, such as Coral Polge, author of *Living Images,* have brought the world of spirit alive. While most of her portraits of the deceased were instantly recognized, one was not:

However, this lady liked the picture that much that she took it home and hung it in the hallway of her house. It was a few months later when new neighbors moved in next door, which followed by a visit of the new neighbor. On entering the hallway, the visitor exclaimed, "Where on earth did you get that picture of my father?"[4]

Clairvoyant, Geoffrey Hodson would agree spirit works in miraculous ways. The author of *The Brotherhood of Angels and Men* believes that there are many types of angels – chief among them, guardian angels, ceremonial, and angels of beauty and art. Hodson suggests wearing these colors for each group:

Angel Colors[5]

Groups of Angels	Colors to Be Worn
Guardian angels of the home	Rose and soft green
Healing angels	Deep sapphire blue
Angels of maternity and birth	Sky blue
Ceremonial angels	White
Angels of music	White
Nature angels	Apple green
Angels of beauty and art	Yellow

There are so many guides who wish to assist us, and a multitude of ways of tuning into their presence. In addition to coming through dreams, meditation, mental or physical mediumship, they may show up with signs. Sometimes just finding a penny can be an indicator spirit is trying to get your attention. Why? A penny proclaims an important message from our spirit friends – "In God we Trust." However your spirit guide makes his or her presence known, welcome each into your band of spirits. Call on them for protection and guidance, and most of all, believe it is possible to make contact with guides. They are after all only a thought or dream away.

Types of Guides

Loved Ones	Parents, grandparents, deceased children, aunts, uncles, and cousin still love us, as do our departed friends. Often they bring validation messages to show they are with us, as well as encouragement.
Spirit Workers	These guides are attracted to us by our work. A writer may attract other deceased writers; a nurse, departed doctors; or a minister, spirit philosophers.
Temporary Guides	These guides come in on an emergency basis, such as the spirit of a mechanic when your car breaks down.
Protectors	Often American Indians and other strong spirits come in for protection.
Joy Guide	Children and child-like beings try to lighten our mood.
Gate Keepers	These spirits keep order in the séance room allowing only one spirit through at a time.
Spirit Teachers	Highly evolved souls and master teachers, such as doctors and philosophers come back to teach higher knowledge.
Spirit Chemist	Master spirit chemists and doctors come through to adjust the chemistry of the medium for spirit communication.
Ascendant Masters	Master guides, such as Jesus, Saint Germain, and El Moyra who work for humanity.
Angels	Spiritual beings who have never incarnated, but remain close to the earth to assist mankind. They are always positive.

Meditation for Spiritual Guidance

Do the exercise in a quiet place when you have an hour to yourself. Turn off the phone and place a pen and a notebook at your side. Have another person slowly read this exercise to you.

In your mind's eye, go to your favorite place to relax. This may be the beach or your own backyard. See yourself relaxing in this place.

Visualize every detail of the place – sight, sound, touch, even the taste. You are totally relaxed. Very, very relaxed.

Take a moment and imagine a white light just above your head. Visualize this white light shining above your head and gently coming down over your face, shoulders, chest, arms, hips, legs, and feet. Feel the protective warmth, gently go down your body from your head to your shoulders, to your chest, hips, legs to the bottoms of your feet. You are totally surrounded by brilliant protective white light.

In a moment – at the count of three– your guide will join you.

One: You are peaceful.
Two: You are excited about seeing your guide. On the count of three but not before, you will see your guide.
Three: Your guide is right in front. Take a moment and look down at the guide's feet. What do the feet look like? Slowly go up the body. What type of clothes does the guide have on? See or feel every detail of your guide. Take a moment to tune in.

Now describe your guide in detail. What does your guide look like? Does the guide have a name or symbol to give to you?

Pause

Your guide has a message for you – a very vital message. Take the next three minutes to tune into this message which will help you at this time in your journey here on the earth plane. (At this point, play some soft, New Age music for three minutes.)

Pause three minutes.

Now that you have received the guidance, thank the guide for being with you today. Send love from your heart to the guide. On the count of seven you will awaken and remember every detail of your session. You

Chief Crazy Horse

will be able to write all the details clearly and easily. The more you write, the more you remember.

One: You are rested.
Two: You are beginning to wake up.
Three: You will remember all details of your guide's message to you.
Four: You feel well and happy.
Five: You feel as if you have slept for eight hours.
Six: You are alert. You feel energy in your body.
Seven: You are fully awake. Eyes wide open.

End Notes

1. James Van Praagh, *Talking to Heaven,* Penguin Books, New York, NY, 1997, page 46.
2. www.angelfire.com/ok/SilverBirch/Tcon.html.
3. Frederick Harding, *Why American Indians Are Spirit Guides?* Stowe Memorial Foundation, Lily Dale NY 1940, page 5.
4. psychictruth.info/Medium_Coral_Polge.htm.
5. Geoffrey Hodson, *The Brotherhood of Angels and Man*, Theosophical Publishing House, Wheaton, IL 1982, page 82.

Suggested Reading

Ted Andrews, *How to Meet and Work with Spirit Guides*
Sylvia Browne. *Contacting Your Spirit Guide*
Robert Chaney. *Mediums and Their Development*
Sonia Choquette. *Ask Your Guides*
Rose Vanden Eynden. *So You Want to Be a Medium*

Nine

Development Circles

Teachers open the door, but you must enter by yourself.

~ Chinese Proverb

The Spiritualist tradition of development circles has produced some excellent mediums, such as Rev. Anne Gehman and James Van Praagh. Gehman studied with Wilbur Hull at Camp Cassadaga in Florida, while Van Praagh attended Brian Hurst's circle in Los Angeles, California. In each case, they attended weekly meditation sessions lead by a veteran medium who was dedicated to Spiritualism, "the Science, Philosophy, and Religion of continuous life, based upon the demonstrated fact of communication, by means of mediumship, with those who live in the Spirit World."[1]

Ever since Brian Hurst tutored James Van Praagh as a medium, Hurst has had many requests to do the same for others. His advice to those who wish to be mediums is to form a circle with like-minded friends.

> When you make that appointment with the other side, and the spirit world sees that you are totally sincere, a band of helpers gradually assembles. They check the energy of each sitter in the group and review their potential.[2]

This process can take some time. It is not unusual to attend a circle for several years to hone clairsentience, clairaudience, and clairvoyant skills. Usually, a circle is made up of six to twelve people who are sincere in their desire to develop mediumship. It is important that the members are harmonious, responsible, and dedicated. Many groups continue for years. However, groups that disband often do so because the members lack discipline and dedication. Remember, spirit guides keeps their weekly appointments, and we should do the same. It is also a good idea for people to arrive early, as late-comers may disrupt the vibration. Also, once meditation begins, the door to the séance room should be firmly closed – late sitters must wait in a designated area until meditation is over, and then they can enter. Once the group is established, use discretion when inviting new members because even one negative participant can lower the energy of the entire group.

Once the group is established, it is important to screen new-comers. When one is suitable, allow him/her a trial period of two or three visits to decide if the group is for the person and vice-versa. Be patient for it does take time and dedication to develop a harmonious circle needed to communicate with the Spirit World.

The group should meet at the same time and place each week. This helps to build up the vibrations. While it is preferable to meet in a church, some groups do meet in homes. If possible, try to use the same home each time, as it is helpful to dedicate the room to spirit with sacred pictures, incense, and even crystals strategically placed to increase the energy. It is also important to turn off cell phones and telephones, and make sure there are no disturbances. In Spiritualist churches, usually a certified medium runs the group. When no veteran medium is available, the leader can be a minister, healer, or the member of the group who has the most experience.

Jane Roberts (1929 – 1984), for example, was not a trained medium or healer, but was very interested in the subject. In 1963, she and her husband, Robert Butts, began to experiment with a Ouija board as part of Roberts' research, *How to Develop Your ESP Power* (1966). It wasn't long before the couple began receiving messages on the Ouija board: On December 3, 1963, Robert F. Butts asked the questions, while his wife, Jane Roberts, placed her fingers on the pointer. Soon an entity by the name of Frank Withers spelled out his name. He told the couple that he had lived in Elmira, New York, on State Street, and had died in 1942. Furthermore, he was a teacher, and his wife's last maiden name was Ursula Alteri.[3] "Frank Withers agreed to be Jane's guide, however he preferred to use the name "Seth."

Seth turned out to be a sensible guide, open to channeling for Roberts' psychic development circle. He advised the group:

> Do not overestimate or underestimate your own messages, whether you receive them through the Ouija board, automatic writing, or voice communication. If the material is valid, it will prove itself out through time, through its own quality and accumulation.[4]

Jane Roberts taught ESP to a group in her living room for eight years, and channeled Seth for twenty-one years. However, she is best remembered for her many channeled books – with *The Nature of Personal Reality*, required reading for Roberts' new students.

Jane Roberts made her classes fun and open to all students. Other mediums may prefer a closed circle. In any case, mediums all have their own style of teaching. The format is usually the same. The leader begins with a prayer, sometimes singing or a lecture on mediumship. Then there is break and the chairs are arranged in a circle for meditation in the dark. During the meditation, spirit will be present. The meditation portion should last from twenty minutes up to one hour. During this period, it is the job of the medium to identify spirits present in the room.

The author observed this process firsthand when she was a member of the Boston Spiritualist circle of Rev. Gladys Custance (1900-1988) and her husband Rev. Kenneth Custance (1904-2004). Mrs. Custance would go into trance during meditation and her guide, a Hindu dubbed "the Professor" would lead the mediation. The medium always advised students to relax, reminding them often "Tension shuts the door." Once the group was relaxed and in a congenial mood, the Custances would work on raising the vibrations. Frequently, Kenneth Custance, a professional musician would play his harp and lead the group in affirmations such as "God is Love" to the tune of "Silent Night." The harp music lifted the vibration as did the positive messages.

Next, the lights would be turned off and the room made as dark as possible. Professor would come through Mrs. Custance, a trance channeled, with messages of encouragement. Then she advise students: "Give impressions as they come to you." Someone might then comment on the change in temperature or a blue light in the room. The teachers would let the student know if their impression was correct. Sometimes, messages were given by the Custances. For example, Mrs. Custance might say, "I have someone here with the name Bill." A student might reply, "Yes, that's the name of my brother who passed over last year." Once Mrs. Custance heard the voice of the sitter, she would continue the communication from spirit. It was necessary to hear the voice of the sitter, as spirit works off voice vibration.

Often phenomena such as the scent of roses or flashes of light would be seen in the séance room Sometimes students reported feeling a pressure on the head, much like that of a helmet – a sure sign spirit was opening the crown chakras and third eyes of the student mediums At the close of the meditation session the energy would drop down; Gladys Custance would invariably ask: "Did anyone feel a change of forces?" – which was her way of letting the students know that the spirits had departed for the evening.

While the Custances held informal séances, the formal séance is back in style. A formal séance is usually limited to twelve participants, seated around a table. Make sure that the room is as quiet as possible – telephone disconnected. Put a tape recorder with fresh batteries in the center of the table to record messages, and a glass of water should be placed in front of the medium and each of the sitters. The water will act as a conductor for psychic energy, as well as a thirst quencher. Once the medium has a established rapport, the séance can begin with a phrase such as, "Spirit, do you have any messages for us?"

Wait patiently for spirit to come through the medium. It is important to allow spirits to come in at their own pace. Often, sitters will report that they feel a change of energy or a change in the atmosphere at this point. Remember spirits of our loved ones and guides exist on the higher plane and they have to lower and adjust their vibration to communicate with us. Conversely, through mediation we need to raise our vibrations and adjust for spirit communication. Spirits are attracted to us through our vibration.

Spirits often like to visit their neighbors. British medium, Muriel Tennant was surprised by a message given during a Spiritualist message service from a local farm boy who had died many years before:

> He wishes you to tell his mother not to visit his grave every week and put flowers there. It's a waste of good money, because he is not there.[5]

Muriel Tenant, who was attending the church for the first time, was dumbfounded when the medium mother's name was Mickleburgh and his name was Percy Webster."[6] Everything the medium said was true. She had indeed known a Percy who had lost his life in a tragic farm accident. Later, Muriel Tennant became a medium and tutor at the Arthur Findlay College. Her advice to students: "Allow spirit to contact you."

While teachers such as Muriel Tennant can be helpful in developing mediumship, some students work on their own. Such was the case for Ivy Northage. When her husband, Stanley, read how Sir Arthur Conan-Doyle sat in the dark on a regular basis to develop his mediumship, he urged Ivy to do the same. It wasn't long before Ivy Northage went into trance and her Chinese guide came through.

> Chan told Stanley that if he would play his part by continuing to sit regularly with me, he would provide the instruction for the training of my mediumship.[7]

Stanley readily agreed to take notes. Ivy Northage went on to become an excellent trance medium through Chan's guidance. She is also realistic about the relationship:

> While I have never done anything Chan has asked me not to, I have on occasion been extremely tired and I know that effects my work. When I am tired, it is as though Chan has difficulty in finding the words in my brain.[8]

Most mediums, such as Ivy Northage, sit for mental mediumship, however, some prefer to sit for physical mediumship. In 1993, two couples in Scole, England, decided to meet for the purpose of unfolding physical mediumship. Later, three others joined their circle. For the next five years, Robin and Sandra Foy, Diana and Allan Bennett, Mimi, Ken, and Bernette met weekly in a dark room for the intention of physical mediumship. Almost immediately, Diana went into trance and the voice of their main guide, Manu, came through with these words of encouragement:

> The team of beings I represent is made up of many thousands of minds from many other realms of existence. We will be working with your group to provide very tangible evidence of these other realms.[9]

The Scole group began with traditional methods of physical mediumship development which is to use a light-weight aluminum trumpet as a megaphone for spirit voices. They formed a circle and placed an aluminum trumpet on the table in the middle. By April, they were getting some phenomena around the trumpet:

> They experienced clicks, whispers, and an incredible coldness. The trumpet fell over into the lap of one of the sitters, but this time, it was more controlled.[10]

Eventually, other spirit guides such as Patrick MeKenna, Raji, Mrs. Bradshaw, Edward Mathews, and spirit scientists, William, Albert, Joseph, and Edwin joined the group.

The results were amazing. Symbols and handwritten messages appeared on factory-sealed, unopened film, as well as spirits who gave instruction on how to build complex devices for spirit communication. The group was investigated by Montague Keen, Arthur Ellison, and David Fontana from the Society for Psychical Research in 1999 with favorable results:

> In the course of over twenty sittings the investigators were unable to detect any direct indication of fraud or deception, and encountered evidence favoring the hypothesis of intelligent forces, whether originating in the human psyche or from discarnate sources, able to influence material objects and to convey associated meaningful messages, both visual and aural.[11]

Due to previous mediumship training, the Scole circle was able to develop quickly, this example is not typical of physical mediumship. Most physical mediums sit for many years

Rev. Gladys Custance
and Rev. Kenneth Custance

to develop their gifts. For instance, Rev. Hoyt Robinette sat in daily mediation for fifteen years to develop his ability to produce spirit writing on cards and Stewart Alexander, a materialization medium, sat in a circle for thirteen years before any physical phenomena occurred!

Stewart Alexander became interested in physical mediumship when he read Arthur Findlay's book *On the Edge of the Etheric*, which included transcripts of many of medium John Sloane's trumpet séances. Two years later, Alexander joined a weekly development circle. Every Monday evening, he would sit in total darkness which is necessary for the production of ectoplasm:

> The spirit people are believed to extract it from the nose, mouth, ear, or solar plexus of the medium. At that stage (beginning), it is said to have the consistency of smoke or liquid, but in an instance can be converted to something with the molecular structure as substantial as steel.[12]

Since the group was sitting for physical development, they placed an aluminum trumpet in the center of the circle in the hope that enough ectoplasm would be produced to move the trumpet through the mechanism of ectoplasm rods. When this occurs, the trumpet becomes an instrument to amplify spirit voices so everyone in the room can hear them. After thirteen years, Stewart had a breakthrough with his own trumpet mediumship. While sitting at the dining room table with a trumpet between him and another sitter, Kath, he became unconscious and his guide took over:

> White Feather – my guide – had asked for the light to be switched off, and a few minutes later, for the first time, the trumpet had risen into the air, and his voice had been heard to issue directly from it.[13]

Whether you wish to sit for mental or physical mediumship, here are some basic rules:

One: Work with a qualified medium.

Two: Choose sincere and dedicated people for the development circle.

Three: Decide on what type of mediumship your circle will pursue.

Four: Meet weekly at the same time and place.

Five: Use the same format each week – prayer or invocation of spirit followed by an inspiration talk. Then take a break. Meditate with soft music or in silence. Often beginners do best with a short period of meditation, while advanced students may meditate for an hour. End with a closing prayer.

Six: Be patient. Development takes time and dedication.

Seven: Remain positive. Refrain from gossip and do not discuss spirit messages outside the circle. Remember: "What is said in the circle should remain in the circle."

End Notes

1. National Association of Spiritualist Churches.
2. Brian Hurst, *Heaven Can Help*, iUniverse, New York, NY, 2007, page 211.
3. Jane Roberts, *How to Develop ESP*, Lifetime Books, Hollywood, FL, 1997, pages 14-16.
4. Jane Roberts, *How to Develop ESP*, Lifetime Books, Hollywood, FL, 1997 page 33.
5. Muriel Tennant, *As I See It*, Chameleon International, Spauding, England,1988, page 23.
6. Muriel Tennant, *As I See It*, Chameleon International, Spauding, England,1988, page 23.
7. Ivy Northage, *While I Remember*, Light Publishing, London, England,1999, pages 49-50.
8. Ivy Northage, *While I Remember*, Light Publishing, London, England, 1999, page 198.
9. Grant and Jane Solomon, *The Scole Experiment*, Champion Books, Essex England, pages 26-27.
10. Grant and Jane Solomon, *The Scole Experiment*, Champion Books, Essex England, page 38.
11. www.afterlife101.com/Scole_1.html.
12. Stewart Alexander, *An Extraordinary Journey*, Saturday Night Publications, Beaconsfield, England, page 31.
13. Stewart Alexander, *An Extraordinary Journey*, Saturday Night Publications, Beaconsfield, England, page 48.

Suggested Reading

Stewart Alexander. *An Extraordinary Journey*
Harry Boddington. *The University of Spiritualism*
Raymond Buckland. *Doors to Other Worlds*
Robert G. Chaney. *Mediums and the Development of Mediumship*
Harry Edwards. *A Guide for the Development of Mediumship*
Rose Vanden Eynden. *So You Want to Be a Medium*
Brian Hurst. *Heaven Can Help*
Ivy Northage. *While I Remember*
Elizabeth Owens. *Spiritualism and Clairvoyance for Beginners*
Jane Roberts. *How to Develop Your ESP Power*
Gordon Smith. *Developing Mediumship*
Grant and Jane Solomon. *The Scole Experiment*

Ten

Psychometry, Photograph Readings, and Billets

Learn from yesterday, live for today, and hope for tomorrow.

~Albert Einstein

Mediums frequently employ several methods to make a connection with spirit. Chief among them are psychometry, photograph reading, and billets. Psychometry is derived from the Greek word for soul which is "psyche" and "metron" which is Greek for measure. The term "psychometry" was coined by Dr. J.R. Buchanan in 1842. Buchanan believed that every object, scene, or event that has occurred has left a psychic imprint or its unique astral light:

> Just as a photograph may be taken on film or plate and remain invisible until it has been developed, so may those psychometric photographs remain impalpable until the developing process has been applied. That which can bring them to light is the psychic faculty and mind of the medium.[1]

Professional mediums use psychometry to make a quick connection to the sitter when doing a reading. According to medium, George Winslow Plummer:

> By holding such an object in his hands, and giving close attention to the same, a consciousness arises similar to inspiration, and tells a story foreign to one's previous knowledge, and from this the history of the object can be gleaned.[2]

The benefits from psychometry are many. They include finding lost objects and missing people; tuning into past, present, and future; as well as contacting spirit. One of the world's most famous psychometrists, Stefan Ossowiecki, has used his psychic gifts to locate both lost objects and missing people. In 1935, he was asked to describe the contents in a package. "Ossowiecki touched the package and concentrated. 'Volcanic minerals,' he said. 'There is something here that pulls me to other worlds, to another planet.' Oddly, he also sensed sugar. Inside the package was a meteorite encased in a candy wrapper."[3]

British medium, Estelle Roberts, was also an exceptional psychometrist. When Mr. Ewart Dudley placed a sealed envelope in front of her, she felt a piece of folded textile. When asked for the message written on the needle work, Estelle Roberts felt the spirit of a woman take her hand to trace:

COME UNTO ME ALL YE THAT LABOR AND ARE HEAVY
LADEN AND I WILL GIVE YOU REST. MARY BAKER[4]

She correctly identified the needlework and quickly added "also in the envelope are two lace fronts which I used to wear with my low-necked blouses. One is square and the other triangular in shape. There is also a narrow strip of hand-worked lace which was done by my mother, your grandmother."[5] When they opened the envelope, lo and behold, there was a picture of Dudley's mother – the spirit who had taken the medium's hand to trace the quote from Mary Baker Eddy!

Joan Grant (1907 – 1989) also had unusual experiences with psychometry when she placed a fragment of the Egyptian pyramid over her forehead. She immediately saw pictures as she recalled a past life as Sekeeta. Soon, she developed "far memory" and was able to piece together her life as a princess who became a "winged pharaoh." In 1937, she published her classic book, *Winged Pharaoh*.

Not only does psychometry work when placing an object on the forehead, but on the solar plexus as well. For instance, Dr. Haddock of London placed Miss Gleason into trance. When objects were placed on her solar plexus, she was able to correctly identify then. She was also able to give simple medical clairvoyance when in hypnosis.

Mediums, such as Lenore Piper (1857-1950), often ask for objects belonging to the dead to establish contact.

According to researcher, E.M. Sidgwick in 1915, Piper said that, 'When a person wears or handles an object, it seems to become infused with something similar to magnetic power, which from then on surrounds the object and enables a medium to obtain information about the person.'[6]

Piper was best known for her deep trance mediumship with spirit guides such as Dr. Phinuit, the Imperator, and George Pelham. Her sessions were particularly evidential, such as one given for Judge Frost of Cambridge, Massachusetts:

> While in trance, Lenore rose from her chair, walked to a table in the center of the room, picked up a pencil and paper, wrote rapidly for a few minutes, and, handing the written paper to a member of the circle, she returned to her seat.[7]

Judge Frost was thrilled to receive a message from his departed son.

Psychometry, such as used by Lenore Piper, is a simple procedure. Start by working with a stranger. Ask for a personal object such as a watch or a ring. Metal seems to hold the energy well. If a woman arrives without any jewelry, ask for her tube of lipstick since it is an object that one doesn't share. For gentlemen without a watch, ask for a wallet. If absolutely nothing is available to hold (which is rare) have the sitter put a piece of paper between their hands for a few minutes and then hold the paper. Avoid keys for psychometry unless you are sure the sitter never lends them out. Also antique jewelry can be confusing, as the original owner may be the one to get the reading, not the sitter.

Once you have the object in your hands, say a prayer such as:

> Loving Father, Divine Mother, may that which is for the sitter's highest good come through. We know with our little will, little can be accomplished, but with God's will all things are possible.

Take seven deep breaths. Relax and allow yourself to tune into the owner. Give out impressions as you receive them. Remember, psychometric impressions may come in the form of feeling, impression, sounds, scents, or even tastes. For example, you might feel the ring belongs to an older female, now deceased. If the sitter acknowledges this to be true, try to gain more rapport with the spirit. Perhaps, you hear the name Rose or smell lilac perfume. You may even see a picture of the female spirit. Finally, ask if there is a message for the sitter? With each session, try to go deeper. For instance, what color eyes did the spirit owner have? How did she pass to spirit?

With patience, even beginners can pick up impression from an object. Objects never lie. It just takes some patience and some compassion to read them.

Flower reading is a variation of psychometry. This most beautiful form of psychometry is sometimes used in churches. The author witnessed this when she visited Camp Chesterfield in Indiana. Rev. Glenda Freeman plucked a yellow gladiola from a bouquet of flowers and turned to her.

She said, "I am holding a flower, but I am impressed to hold it like a pen. I feel you have something to do with writing?" Rev. Freeman was right on target.

Another excellent method of psychic readings akin to psychometry is photograph reading. Nearly everyone receives mental impressions as they look at a photograph. While psychologists pay attention to facial expression, attire, and body language, psychics can go deeper and receive valid impressions. As with psychometry, take a moment to relax, say a prayer and ask for guidance. You may immediately sense the personality and interests, and even receive images from the other side of loved ones. With practice, you can even scan a picture of the body for imbalances. With time and practice, a psychic can be trained to read a person's past, present, and future from a photograph.

After you become adept at psychometry and photograph reading, you may wish to try your hand at billet reading. While the procedure is relatively simple, it does take a fair amount of practice to be accurate. In order to gain experience, assemble a group of friends who are interested in the paranormal for billet readings. Be careful to weed out skeptics, as even one skeptic can pull down the vibrations. Begin with a short discussion of mediumship and billet reading to warm up your audience. Then pass out small slips of paper which the French call billet. If you wish you can use the billet at the end of the chapter.

Have each person write the names of deceased relatives, friends on the other side, and spirit guides that they wish to contact. Each person is to write one question for spirit to answer. Next, tell them to sign their names when they are finished. At this point, spirit will receive their request. Finally, have each person fold the billet and place it in a sealed envelope. Collect the billets on a tray or in a basket. The medium is then securely blind-folded. He or she opens each of the envelopes and holds the billet to gain rapport. At this point, spirit will come in for identification and the medium gives a description of deceased loved ones.

When reading a photograph with more than one person, focus on only one face and cover the others. (Author with mother, Dorothy Marshall, and sister, Barbara.)

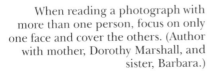

Then the medium will tune into the answer to the sitter's question. Sometimes the medium will just hold the envelope for the billet reading, and then push aside the blind-fold and open the envelope to confirm the accuracy of the message. Originally, billet reading was devised as a test of mediumship and clairvoyance by early Spiritualists who would "mind read" information from slips of paper.

However, while billet reading can be very accurate, it can also be easily faked. By the "one ahead method," the pretend medium simply has a conspirator planted in the audience. After the "performer" pretends to read contents of the first billet, the "plant" jumps up and confirms the message. When the fake medium opens the first envelope to "check" the first billet, he or she has the information for the second billet. The "medium" then pretends to use clairvoyance or mediumship to read the second billet! Just as there are pretenders in all walks of life, it can be discouraging when those professing to be Spiritualists use this method. Fortunately, the vast number of Spiritualists are sincere in their religious beliefs. Nowadays, most billet mediums perform billet readings with heavily sealed blindfolds to avoid any hint of impropriety.

End Notes

1. psychictruthinfo@talktalknet.
2. *A Brief Course in Mediumship* by George Winslow Plummer, page 13.
3. www.spirit writings. com/ Fifty Years a Medium by Estelle Robert.
4. www.spirit writings. com/ Fifty Years a Medium by Estelle Roberts.
5. www.articlesnatch.com/Article/Your-Psychic-Psychometry-Powers.
6. paranexus.org/parapedia/index.php?title=Psychometry.
7. www.fst.org/piper.htm.

Suggested Reading

Ted Andrews. *How to Do Psychic Readings Through Touch*
Joseph Rhodes Buchanan. *Manual of Psychometry: The Dawn of a New Civilization*
Suzy Chiazzari. *Flower Readings*
Sidney Flower. *A Course of Instruction in Development of Power Through Psychometry*
Sepharial. *Psychometry*

Forms for working with sitters follow.

Sitter: _____

Date: _____

Psychometry

1. Hold a small object such as a watch or a ring in your hand. It is best to choose a from a person you do not know.

2. Hold the object to gain rapport. Give impressions as you received them. Try to get some basic impressions. Is the owner male or female, old or young, living or dead, shy or out-going?

3. Now go deeper. What did he or she look like? Describe their style of dress, hair, and eye color. Then go deeper into personality traits and hobbies.

4. Call on your spirit guides to see if there is more information that spirit wishes to share.

5. Now ask the owner, to give you some feedback. What percentage did you get right? A good psychic is usually about eighty-five percent correct.

Notes

_____

_____

_____

_____

_____

_____

_____

Sitter: _____

Date: _____

Photograph Reading

1. Hold a photograph of someone you do not know.

2. As you look into the photograph, gaze into the eyes of the subject to gain rapport. Give impressions as you receive them. Try to get some basic impressions. Is the person alive? If deceased, how did the person die?

3. Now go deeper. What did he or she look like? Describe their style of dress, hair, and eye color. Then go deeper into personality traits and hobbies.

4. Call on your spirit guides to see if there is more information that spirit wishes to share.

5. Now ask the owner to give you some feedback. What percentage did you get right? A good psychic is usually about eighty-five percent correct.

Notes

_____

_____

_____

_____

_____

_____

_____

Billet Procedures

1. Work with a small group of serious mediumship students. Distribute the billets.

2. Instruct each person to write the names of deceased loved ones they wish to contact and one question. Then sign their name. Spirit will receive the message as soon as the billet is signed. Fold the billet and hold it in your hands.

3. Everyone then places their billets in an envelope, seals it, and places the envelops in a basket.

4. Select one envelope. Take a deep breath and relax. Concentrate on the billet. As you mind becomes still, tune into impressions, ideas, or messages from spirit. Open envelope and read the billet. Immediate feedback is very helpful to develop accuracy.

Billet

Write the names of three people in the spirit world that you would like to contact and one question for spirit to answer. Then sign the billet.

1. _____

2. _____

3. _____

Question: _____

_____

Signature: _____

Eleven

Psychic Detectives

Everyone is psychic to some degree, and really successful paranormal investigators, even if they do not realize it, are using their own psychic ability to sense the environment.

~Rosemary Ellen Guiley

Psychic detectives, such as Peter Hurkos, Dorothy Allison, Noreen Renier, Nancy Meyers, Carol Pate, Mary Ellen Rodriquez, Pam Coronado, Christine Holohan, and Allison Dubois often use psychometry to investigates crimes. However they all employ slightly different techniques. For instance, Noreen Renier frequently starts her psychic readings, by holding an article from the victim, while Peter Hurkos holds a sealed envelope containing pictures of the crime scene. Nancy Meyers also requests recent pictures of the crime scene and the victim to make a connection. Dorothy Allison, "the human radio," uses her clairvoyance, while Pam Coronado prefers clairsentience. To gain information, both Carol Pate and Mary Ellen Rodriquez have used dreams along with their clairvoyant skills. Finally, mediums such as Christine Holohan and Allison Dubois contact the spirit of the victim!

While many psychic detectives are born with their gift, the late Peter Hurkos (1911-1988) discovered his ability after falling from a ladder. After surviving a three-day coma, he discovered he could see the unknown. He gained recognition for investigations of the Boston Strangler Murders in the early 1960s and the 1969 Sharon Tate murders. How does Hurkos receive his information on these cases? According to Hurkos, "I see pictures in my mind like a television screen. When I touch something, I can then tell what I see." Hurkos often requested a picture of the murder scene be placed in a sealed envelope. Then he would use psychometry to reconstruct the murders in great detail. In one case, he even visited the grave of a victim to make a psychic connection. His biographer, Norma Lee Browning, claims Hurkos had a ninety percent success rate, while others such as Katherine Rams are more skeptical:

"Hurkos sat in the room where Sharon Tate and her friends had been murdered, envisioning several perpetrators. This was correct, but a good profiler or detective could have spotted that fact."

Much like profilers, psychic detectives, such as Dorothy Allison do provide useful clues to police. When asked how she received the information, Dorothy Allison says she sees flashes of information such as the vision of a small Polish boy who had drowned. Her most famous case was that of Son of Sam murders in New York. Allison gave the police several important leads:

> She drew a very accurate portrait of the killer that looked a lot
> like David Berkowitz. She correctly predicted that the killer
> would be caught because of a parking ticket.[3]

Noreen Renier is another gifted psychic detective, who according to Detective Joseph Uribe of Montana Department of Justice, is "accurate in every detail" in an assault case with details on "where the assault took place, description of the assault, that it was an ambush, that a blue metal building was important in solving the crime. The sketch drawn from Noreen Renier's descriptions was 'perfect.'"[4] No wonder Noreen Renier was invited to lecture at the FBI Academy in Quantico, Virginia, in 1981. She was also called in to investigate the murder of a seventeen year old, Kaitlyn, who had been shot in her car on the night of July 16, 1989. Lois Duncan, her mother was amazed at the amount of information that Noreen Renier was able to obtain with psychometry:

> The psychic held the earrings and necklace that Kaitlyn was
> wearing when she was shot and received impressions of what the
> girl had experienced in her last moments. She also described
> Kaitlyn's movements that night.[5]

Duncan also consulted another psychic detective, Betty Muench, who, through automatic writing, told Duncan that her daughter was angry, knew information regarding a "dangerous situation," that Kaitlyn knew her killer, and "money had changed hands after the murder." Both psychics had been accurate, when "she discovered that Kaitlyn's Vietnamese boyfriend, Dung Nguyen, was involved in an insurance-claim scheme."[6] Even though one man was charged in 1991, the case was dropped due to lack of evidence. Lois Duncan later told the whole story in her book, *Who Killed My Daughter?* In another strange twist to the case, Duncan actually predicted many of the details of her daughter's murder in an earlier book!

Psychic detectives have also helped the police in England. One of the best examples is that of medium, Christine Holohan. Since the police were initially skeptical, she used her skill as a psychometrist to convince the two officers that she was indeed psychic and her visions of the Jacqui Poole murder were real:

> I took the police officer's keys in my hand and instantly receive information and images about his life. I told him that he would need to get the house he was thinking of buying rewired or he would not qualify for a mortgage.[7]

Christine Holohan then gave them the news that brought her to the police station. She told them how she had been contacted by the spirit of a murdered woman, Jacqueline Poole. She not only described the murder scene but seemed to know other pertinent details, such Poole's maiden name, Jackie Hunt, her divorce, and the fact the Poole had just been given a prescription for depression medication.

When pressed for more details, the medium went into trance and contacted the spirit of Jacqui Poole. Jacqui told them, "You have got the right group" rather than, "You had the right man in custody last Monday." Christine Hunt really got the attention of police detective Tony Batters when "she gave a detailed description of the killer and with 'automatic writing' wrote down the name 'Pokie' which we now know to be the killer's nickname.[10] When modern DNA testing was used sixteen years later, justice was served when Pokie was convicted of Jacqui Poole's murder.

While the police are not too interested in psychics, they are impressed by facts. Christine got the approval of veteran detective Tony Batters when she gave him 120 accurate details of the Jacqui Poole murder. Similarly the police have high praise for psychic detective, Nancy Meyers, who assisted the police in finding the whereabouts of three children kidnapped by their father. The psychic told the police the three Harding New Jersey children had been taken to Euless, Texas. Unfortunately, the police arrived only after the father had fled. Nancy then gave the police a second address, Ramona, California, where the children were found. According to Lou Materbone of the Morris County Sheriff's Department:

> If it wasn't for Nancy Weber (psychic), in this case we would not have gotten the (kidnapped) children back ... her insight, her help ... we could not have done it without her.[11]

How does Nancy Meyers do it? Well, she starts with pictures of the victims and maps of their home, work, or school, and the date of the last time they were seen alive. She sometime asks for samples of handwriting. Information beyond that which is requested, Meyers considers distracting. She then does a "cold reading" and reports back to the police

Carol Pate is another psychic detective with a strong record of success. In 1991, she was chosen as the top psychic in the United States by the Tokyo Broadcast System in Japan. The great-granddaughter of a Cherokee medicine man, Pate was a born psychic. Her first case? At twelve, she saw clairvoyantly the murder of a classmate who had been accidentally shot in the back. Ever since then, Pate has been a valuable asset to law enforcement. Early in her career, Carol Pate studied with famed San Francisco medium, Florence Becker (1892-1970) pastor of the Golden Gate Spiritualist Church. Rev. Becker was a gifted clairvoyant, billet reader, and trumpet medium. In 1913, she began to precipitate painting on canvas. While Florence Becker was in trance, her sitters would sing the French National Anthem over and over again for up to two hours. Then all would hear a clap which was a signal that the painting was finished.

> They could turn on the lights or open the curtains and look at the painting then, but were told to cover it with a black, light-proof cloth afterwards and keep it out of the light for a year. After that, they could display it.[12]

There are twenty seven of these paintings on display at the Golden Gate Church in San Francisco.

With such an illustrious teacher, it is no wonder that Pate developed into an excellent psychic. Her ability to pick up clues is uncanny. For instance, when she was recently asked the location of kidnap victim, the word "ridge" came into her head. It turned out Ridge Road was the main route to the kidnap site. While skeptics claim this information could have come from consulting a map, the author has found Carol Pate to be very accurate.[13] On one occasion, she correctly predicted a trip to Brazil which was definitely not planned at the time. Yet within the year, the author went to Brazil to research John of God!

Carol Pate has been featured on the *Psychic Detectives* TV show, as well as another psychic, Mary Ellen Rodriquez. Medium Mary Ellen Rodriquez has also been uncannily accurate in her readings and psychic investigations. For example, when family man, Darryl Cozart, did not come home from work one night, his wife suspected the worst. Later, the spirit of Darryl Cozart contacted medium and shop owner Mary Ellen Rodriquez. He urged her to tell the police officer that visited her store about his death.

> She tells him Darryl is dead, he's been shot, there's something around his neck and his body will be found in a marshy area. Darryl's spirit becomes Mary Ellen's constant companion and the driving force behind her own search for Darryl's body.[13]

The police eventually catch Cozart's murder – a jealous husband of one of his coworkers!

Allison Dubois is another accurate psychic, She has been thoroughly researched at the Human Energy Systems Laboratory by University of Arizona with positive results. The Phoenix-area clairvoyant/spiritualist's work with law enforcement is the basis for the television series *Medium*. The author of *Don't Kiss Them Good Bye* says that she worked with the Glendale Arizona Police Department, the Texas Rangers, and a County Attorney's office in the Homicide Bureau. What advice does she have for those who wish to contact their own deceased loved ones? Dubois' advice:

> Don't force it and be sure to tell the deceased what you need from them not as a challenge but from your heart. It also has to be within their power, like if you requested a 'visit' from them in a dream.[14]

Just as many tune into *Medium* based on Allison Dubois, so others enjoy *Sensing Murder* which features psychic detective, Pam Coronado. It is interesting to note Coronado began her career as a psychic detective because of a vivid dream which provided her with information needed to find a missing California woman. She originally shunned dreams and even consulted psychic, Alan Vaughan, regarding nightmares that plagued her. The noted author of *Dreams Telepathy, Patterns of Prophecy*, and *Incredible Coincidences* encouraged Coronado to work with dreams productively, instead of avoiding them. In 2000, Alan Vaughn asked his student to participate in a documentary.

> Pam's work later caught the attention of the Sci Fi channel who wanted to put her to the test, live, on camera. Again wanting to make her parapsychologist mentor proud, she rose to the challenge and earned a ninety percent accuracy rating from a skeptical detective on Sci Fi's *Proof Positive*.[15]

Becoming a top psychic detective took time – twelve years. However, today Pam Coronado is proud that she has developed her psychic skills to the point where she "can make a difference in an investigation."

While Allison Dubois and Pam Coronado seem to be enjoying their careers, a psychic detective is not without its perils, as Etta Smith found out in 1980. After she heard on the radio a woman was missing, she began to receive very strong impressions of the nurse being dumped in a canyon. The Los Angeles shipping clerk said. "It was like someone was talking to me."[17] Upset and wishing to be of help, Smith decided to report her impressions of the location of the missing

Noreen Renier, Psychic Detective

woman, Melanie Uribe, to the police. Unfortunately, instead receiving thanks, Etta Smith was thrown in jail as suspect. The California authorities simply could not fathom how Etta received her deadly accurate information. Fortunately, a jury did, and awarded Etta Smith $24,000 for wrongful arrest!

End Notes

1. www.peterhurkos.com/peter_biography.htm 2http://www.trutv.com/library/crime/criminal_mind/forensics/psychics/9.html.
3. http://eteponge.blogspot.com/2007/08/veridical-cases-of-psychic-detective.html.
4. www.victorzammit.com/articles/psychicdetectives.htm.
5. www.trutv.com/library/crime/criminal_mind/forensics/psychics/4.html.
6. www.trutv.com/library/crime/criminal_mind/forensics/psychics/4.html.
7. Christine Holohan, A Whisper From An Angel, Random House, New York, NY, page 48.
8. www.tonyyouens.com/ruislip_murder.htm.
9. www.tonyyouens.com/ruislip_murder.htm.
10. www.tonyyouens.com/ruislip_murder.htm.
11. www.victorzammit.com/articles/psychicdetectives.htm.
12. www.spiritualistresources.com/cgi-bin/great/index.pl?read=131.
13. www.liveandtimes.com/psychic-investigators-darryl-cozart--0400-0430pm.html.
14. arkansasmatters.com/fulltext?nxd_id=331905.
15. www.allisondubois.com/index.php/Frequent-Questions/.
16. www.pamcoronado.com/aboutPam.htm.
17. www.victorzammit.com/articles/psychicdetectives.htm.

Psychic Detective Photograph Reading

1. Hold a photograph of a missing person. Try local newspapers to gain practice.

2. As you look into the photograph, gaze into the eyes of the subject to gain rapport. Give impressions as you received them. Try to get some basic impressions. Is the person alive? If deceased, how did the person die?

3. Now go deeper. Take a moment and count from one to seven, as you reach, you may see the location of the missing person.

4. Call on your spirit guides to see if there is more information that spirit wishes to share.

5. Now check the news daily. When the missing person is located, what percentage did you get right? A good psychic detective is usually about eighty-five percent correct.

Notes

_____

_____

_____

_____

_____

_____

_____

_____

Twelve

Opening the Third Eye and Reading Auras

It is one of the commonest of mistakes to consider that the limit of our power of perception is also the limit of all there is to perceive.

~C.W. Leadbeater

Psychic detectives, along with and Spiritualist mediums, use clairvoyance to connect with spirit. While developing clairvoyance takes time and patience, the rewards are many. Chief among its benefits is the ability to see the faces of loved ones and spirit guides. In addition, psychic detectives use clairvoyance to "see" the crime scene of the crime and tune into the mind and image of the criminal. Medical mediums, who usually work with physicians, can visually enter the body for diagnosis and treatment. Some extraordinary clairvoyants, such as C.W. Leadbeater, were even able to peer inside an atom before powerful microscopes were invented. When scientists did look into the atom, its structure was exactly as Leadbeater noted in *Occult Chemistry* which was published in 1908.

C.W. Leadbeater was a Theosophist who would have agreed with the healer, Olga Worrall, that clairvoyance should not be taken lightly or used in an unethical manner. As Worrall explained:

> The clairvoyant gift may be small or great in each of us, it can however be developed. It can be tried, tested, recognized, used. But it is not a childish toy or a cocktail-hour sideshow.[1]

What then are the best and most judicious methods to develop clairvoyance? In the East, meditation is recommended because, with regular practice, it will naturally open the sixth chakra which governs clairvoyance. Sometimes the process is even hastened as in the case of Lobsang Rampa, author of *The Third Eye*. According to Rampa, his master teacher drew a small hole, and drilled into his forehead to open his third eye:

> A very hard, clean sliver of wood had been treated by fire and herbs and was slid down so that it just entered the hole in my head. I felt a stinging, tickling sensation apparently in the bridge of my nose. It subsided and I became aware of subtle scents which I could not identify. Suddenly there was a blinding flash.

Lama Mingyar Dondup then told the initiate:

> You are now one of us, Lobsang. For the rest of your life you will see people as they are and not as they pretend to be.[1]

Few would be willing to undergo such a procedure; most would prefer the slower, systematic development of the inner eye through meditation. For in the East, it is believed sidhis such as clairvoyance unfold as the student is ready.

Of course, some people are born with their third eye already open. In fact, most babies are clairvoyant, but lose this faculty as they incarnate more fully into their bodies. Often young children have spirit play mates – that is until their parents tell them these spirit children are not real!

Occasionally a child's clairvoyance is so strong it will stay with him throughout life. Such was the case for young boy in Cyril Scott's book, *The Boy Who Saw True*. This diary penned by a child in 1885 tells about his ability to see and hear spirits. It took him a while to realize other people were not able to see auras and spirits. For example, he saw the spirit of man possessing a woman, Miss Salt. The clairvoyant child explained:

> She (Miss Salt) has short hair like what papa calls a rat's back, and talks in a manly voice and has an old gentleman inside her (via her aura). I thought this rather funny, (queer) so while we were sitting in the drawing room before tea with Cousin Agnes, I said, "Why have you got an old gentleman sticking to you?" Then she jumped and said, "God bless my soul. What does that little boy mean?"

Naturally, the psychic child suffered many indignities, yet he still wished to help others and allowed his wife to publish his diary after his death.

It is unusual to see spirit in full view, especially in the daylight as the boy who saw true. When you first experience clairvoyance, you will see tiny pin point lights – often white, blue, or purple about the size of a dime. This is more likely to occur in a dark room as clairvoyants see better in darkness. With consistent practice, the full outline of spirit appears. Only experienced clairvoyants see the whole spirit all the time

Researchers, such as Dr. Rick Stassman and Dr. Samuel Sagan, investigated clairvoyance. They have placed the third eye with the pineal gland which is located between the two hemispheres of the brain. According to the Rosicrucians:

> To regain contact with the inner worlds, it is necessary to establish the connection of the pineal gland and the pituitary body with the cerebrospinal nervous system, and to reawaken the pituitary body and the pineal gland.

The Chinese Taoists also believe in activating the third eye. Often they advise qigong students to focus attention on the point between the eyebrows with the eyes closed when doing postures. With this practice, the students gain the ability to reach advance stages of meditation. Apparently, everyone has the potential to activate the pineal gland and to open the third eye. While some prefer meditation, others such as yogis utilize the candle meditation given at the end of the chapter to stimulate clairvoyance.

Basically, spiritual meditation raises the life force or kundalini energy which lies dormant at the base of the spine to the level of the third eye. Some, such as Madame Helena Blavatsky, have unusual clairvoyant contact with the Masters. For instance, once in Paris, she was told by her Master to go to an apartment in the city with the little money she had in her possession. She knocked on the door just in time to save an impoverished man from committing suicide. In addition to great clairvoyant powers, Madame Blavatsky had the ability to levitate, engage in astral travel, and materialize objects. She was also a prolific channeler of such books as *Iris Unveiled* and *The Secret Doctrine*.

Most clairvoyants begin by seeing colors around people's heads. Edgar Cayce, a medical clairvoyant, saw auras all the time. One day as he was about to get on an elevator, he saw the occupants had no auras. Upset, he stepped back. Seconds later, the elevator cable snapped and everyone on the elevator died. While the absence of an aura can indicate imminent death, a large aura may indicate increased influence or fame.

Edgar Cayce often gave aura readings for his clients seeking advice. For example, he gave this reading to a middle-aged teacher whose aura was grey tinged with white. Cayce's advice?

> You have become fearful of the thing to which you have entrusted your inner self. There arise some smears of white coming from your higher intellectual self and from your spiritual intents and purposes.[4]

Cayce wisely advised the woman to focus on her positive attributes by broadening her intellect and spiritual intentions. Cayce gave this advice to a young nurse with green and blue with occasional streaks of red in her aura, which represents anger:

> I would not want to be around you when you do the streaking (of red) and most people who know you feel the same way, for when you let go, it is quite a display of temper.[5]

He went on to compliment her healing ability (green) and helpfulness to others.

From Edgar Cayce's aura reading, you can see colors in the aura tell much about the individual personality and temperament. Red shows vitality; however, too much red or red streaks show the potential for anger and even rage. Frequently, red is strong in the auras of athletes and those who engage in physical labor. When there is a lot of red in the aura, the person is prone to make quick decisions.

Like red, orange is a high energy color. Orange can indicate pride and is a good money-making color. Successful people from sales to the performing art have some orange in their aura. They just know if you believe in yourself, others will too! People with an abundance of orange in their auras can get things going. However, too much orange may indicate false pride or stubborn qualities.

Next, yellow is the color of the mind. Teachers, for example may have yellow in their auras. People with a lot of yellow in their aura are seldom still. They are talkative, funny, and good communicators. Pale yellow can show a timid nature, but a bright yellow indicates confidence and a positive attitude.

Green, the middle color of the color spectrum, is next. It is the color of harmony and denotes compassion. Doctors, nurses, and social workers have a lot green in their auras, as do mothers of young children. Often these helpful people can be trusted to care for others. If green is strong in the aura, the person loves nature. However, if there is a "slime" green streak in the aura, watch out for jealousy!

Blue indicates a spiritual quality, ranging from blue-green which likes to help in a practical way to true blue, the color of an idealist to the deep cobalt blue of a clairvoyant. Ministers as well as mediums have blue in their energy fields. Often people with deep blue in their aura are honest and have good judgment. However, sometimes too much blue without any red, orange or yellow for balance can create a recluse.

Finally, purple is the last color and is rarely seen in most auras. It is a color of deep devotion. Edgar Cayce felt purple indicates change and once a decision is made, purple would settle into blue. A light purple can indicate a change is coming, but the person doesn't know it yet, while a deep dark purple indicates there is change of which the individual is fully aware.

Combinations of colors are also important. Many police and firemen have the blue of service combined with red indicating a preference for physical activity. Deep kelly-green combined with cobalt blue may indicate a spiritual or psychic healer. Sometimes if people are depressed, but seeking help, there may be black and purple in equal combinations in their auras. When someone is anxious and unable to make a decision, a psychic may see a red line going up and down several times like red rickrack. When the person does decide, the line will straightened out.

Colors in the Aura

Red	Vitality, physical strength – too much red, anger
Orange	Confidence, pride – too much orange, very sensual
Yellow	Intelligence, reason, sense of humor – pale yellow, timid
Green	Helpful, healing, fair – slime green, jealous
Blue	Idealistic, spiritual – too much blue, reclusive
Dark Blue	Conservative, responsible – overwhelmed by responsibility
Black	Depressed
White	Pure motive

Science has studied the human energy field including aura with some degree of success. For example, Dr. Walter Kilner invented a device to see the aura by using a glass lens covered by a blue die. In 1911, Kilner wrote a book, *The Human Atmosphere* which detailed his experiences. Often, those who use Kilner's photography pick up the out layer of the aura. When a healer's hands are photographed, the aura is often wider and filled with energy. It is also interesting to note, when hands of people who love each other are photographed; their auras may lean toward one another!

Modern aura photography began with the invention of the aura camera in 1970 by Guy Coggins. Nowadays, aura photographers can use his Aura Camera 6000 to capture the aura surrounding the upper portion of the body and actually photograph the colors in the aura. In fact, many aura photographers, such as the late Linda Wiggins photographed not only colors, but spirit figures such as angels behind the subject.

While the aura camera cannot yet capture the faces of spirit, clairvoyants do view spirit faces. When tuning into spirit clairvoyantly, take time to notice the eyes, face, mouth, and hair. How old is the spirit? What clothes are they wearing? When did the spirit person die? Also try to get an initial or a name. Often, even experienced clairvoyants have difficulty getting names. For example, it took Estelle Roberts several tries to get this name: Mahamogalana. "Time after time he spelled out the name, but for some reason I could never get beyond the first six letters – MAHAMO. Six more letter followed these but, try as I would, I could not get them." Fortunately, the sitter, Sir John, knew it was the name of one of Lord Buddha's chief disciples, Mahamogalana.[6]

Typical clairvoyant reading is done with the eyes closed. As the clairvoyant begins to tune into the aura, he or she will describe color, shades, and shapes. Once you have established your clairvoyance, notice how the sitter's aura changes over time. Sometimes people's aura will lighten if their health is diminished. Often, the opposite is true when happiness enters their life. Then the aura is brighter and more expanded. Next, tune into the spirits in the room. Typically, they will line up in back of the medium. As each one comes into view, describe the spirit. Try to place the relationship of the spirit to the sitter and if possible, give an initial or name. Finally ask the spirit if he or she has a message for the sitter.

Aura Exercise

Have a person, (preferably someone who you know little about) stand against a white wall. Take a moment to call on your spirit guides. Say a prayer of protections and then concentrate your gaze on the area just above their head. Notice what colors seem to be there. Take your time. If you do not see colors, close your eyes and try to tune in with intuition. With practice you should be able to see or intuit colors.

You can also measure the aura's size with dowsing rods. First, you must clear the rods. This can easily be done by wiping them with salt water or placing them under a full Moon.

Then program copper dowsing rods for "yes" and "no" signals. For example,

Rev. Charles Webster Leadbeater,
noted clairvoyant and theosophist

if the two rods cross each other, that might means *yes*. If they remain still, that might mean *no*. Then ask your spirit guides "Where is the beginning of the person's aura? Please cross when I reach it." Have the person sit or stand about ten feet in front of you. Then slowly walk forward. As the rods cross, this place is where the aura begins.

End Notes

1. Olga Worrall, *Explore Your Psychic World*, Ariel Press, Columbus OH, 1989, page 17.
2. www.reversespins.com/possession.html.
3. www.rosicrucian.com/zineen/magen120.htm.
4. Edgar Cayce, *Auras*, ARE Press, 1973, page 17.
5. Edgar Cayce, *Auras*, ARE Press, 1973, page 18.
6. http://homepage.ntlworld.com/robert.moss4/articles/roberts.

Suggested Reading

Edgar Cayce. *Auras*
W. E. Butler. *How to Read the Aura and Practice Psychometry, Telepathy, and Clairvoyance*
Eileen Garrett. *Awareness*
C.W. Leadbeater. *Clairvoyance*
Elizabeth Owens. *Spiritualism and Clairvoyance for Beginners*

Thirteen

Medical Clairvoyance

As has been and is understood by the Body, all good, all health, all life comes from God.

~Edgar Cayce
Reading 658-15

From Rev. Andrew Jackson Davis to today's Dr. Norman Shealy, physicians have used clairvoyance for medical diagnosis. Davis was outstanding in the field because he was a clairvoyant first, and then obtained his medical degree so he could legally practice medical clairvoyance in his Boston office at the turn of the century. Dr. Shealy, another innovative physician, chose to use Caroline Myss, a professional psychic, for medical diagnosis. The two first coined the term "medical intuitive" in 1987. Many such as Shealy believe that a medical intuitive can "see" inside objects as well as the body. Other medical clairvoyants believe that they can view energy problems in a person's aura before any physical signs of illness can be detected.

Medical mediums, on the other hand, rely more on spirit doctors for diagnosis and treatment. Andrew Jackson Davis, Edgar Cayce, Harry Edwards, George Chapman, Jose Arigo, Rev. Alex Orbito, John of God, and Steven Upton all give credit for their cures to spirit. Medical clairvoyants are practitioners who use their psychic abilities to attempt to find the cause of a physical or emotional conditions. Sometimes, they are called health intuitives or medical psychics. Some medical clairvoyants use their ability to read the aura or see into the body to describe diseases by stating the symptoms. While it is illegal to diagnose medically, or for that matter to treat a medical condition, a clairvoyant may see a gray spot on a fifty-year-old woman's left breast, and urge the client to see her physician for a medical diagnosis. Sometimes faith healers have this ability as well. For instance, William M. Branham, the founder of the Latter Rain Movement, was able to discern health conditions. Also, Kathryn Kulhman (1907-1976), noted TV evangelist, frequently sensed

107

conditions that needed healing. Those who tuned into her weekly TV program, *I Believe In Miracles,* saw her mystic ability as she made statements such as, "Someone in this row has a heart condition." Faith healers, such as Kathryn Kulhman, often show a psychic streak.

Faith healing in the United States dates back to Phineas Parkhurst Quimby (1802 -1866) who began his healing practice in 1854. Quimby possessed a perceptive and intuitive mind. In the fall of 1859, Quimby opened an office in Portland, Maine. Eventually, he treated over 12,000 patients, which included Warren Felt Evans, a mental healer, Julius and Annette Dresser, organizers of New Thought movement, and Mary Baker Eddy, the founder of Christian Science. Eddy's detractors charged that she stole the idea from Dr. Quimby. Mary Baker Eddy, of course, denied the charge.

In any event Quimby was the first to use "mind cures." He believed totally on the power of the mind. On November 4, 1856, he wrote to a female patient:

> As I told you, every thought contains a substance – either good or bad – and it comes in and makes up a part of your body (or mind); and as the thoughts which are in your system are poisoned, and the poison has come from without – it is necessary to know how to keep them out of your system, so as not to be injured by them.[1]

He was also able to diagnose clairvoyantly at a distance. To Miss B, Dr. Quimby explained that her illness was due to pressure on her neck:

> This makes it heavy, so it bears on the shoulders, cramps the neck, numbs the chest, so that you give way at the pit of the stomach and feel as though you wanted something to hold you up. This cramps the stomach, giving you a gone-feeling at the pit of the stomach. This contraction presses on the bowels and causes a full feeling, at times, and a heaviness about your hips, and a logy feeling when you walk.[2]

Apparently, he also was in the habit of visiting his patient while astral traveling:

> I shall visit you at night while you are sleeping in your bed and use my influence to make you rest well, so you will be able to walk. You need not give yourself any fears of my forsaking you, nor leaving you in the hands of your enemies. I shall watch over you, till you are able to take care of yourself, if my power is able to do it.[3]

The field of medical clairvoyance began with Dr. Andrew Jackson Davis (1826-1910). Davis, a trance medium, whose guide, Galen and Emmanuel Swedenborg, was able to obtain higher spiritual and medical knowledge with great accuracy. For example, when science knew of only seven planets, *The Principles of Nature*, channeled by Davis stated that there were nine planets revolving around the Sun.

He greatly influenced the early development of Spiritualism, particularly in his association of mediumistic revelations with religious principles. His concepts of after-death spheres for departed spirits, which he named "Summerland," are still part of the beliefs of many modern Spiritualists. He also described in detail what happens to the soul at death, and explained spiritualism and other metaphysical phenomena. His scope of knowledge extended to education, health, psychology, philosophy, and government.[4] Davis even predicted the coming of Spiritualism in his notes of March 31, 1848:

> About daylight this morning a warm breathing passed over my face and I heard a voice, tender and strong, saying: "Brother, the good work has begun – behold, a living demonstration is born." I was left wondering what could be meant by such a message.[5]

That very day, Kate and Maggie Fox contacted the spirit of a murdered peddler!

Andrew Jackson Davis was also the first person to diagnose and prescribe cures for individuals while himself in a trance stare about fifty years before Edgar Cayce.

> In his writings about the human body and health, Davis described how the human body was transparent to him in this trance state. Each organ of the body stood out clearly with a special luminosity of its own which greatly diminished in cases of disease. [5]

Dr. Davis was a most compassionate physician often addressing his patients as "Dear Brother." Like Quimby, his beloved healing came from the Divine mind.

> The Divine Mind is the Cause, the Universe is the Effect, and Spirit is the ultimate design.[6]

Later, Edgar Cayce 1877-1945, demonstrated the ability to diagnose and treat illness while in trance. Nearly two thirds of the 14,256 readings that Cayce gave over a period of forty years were for medical conditions.

Edgar Cayce. *Courtesy of the Association* for *Research and Enlightenment*

His guides had told him early on that he would either be very rich or very poor. Unfortunately, the later turned out to be true, and he had to rely on the financial help of others to keep a modest roof over his head. It is interesting to note the times that Cayce sought to use the readings to locate a site to drill for oil, turned out to be financial disaster, yet a year later, another prospector struck oil.

Cayce's spiritual efforts did bear fruit with a legacy of medical, life readings, and spiritual advice. The readings focused on drugless cures such as osteopathy, massage, enhanced spiritual awareness, and mental changes, as well as the use of Castor Oil packs. Two books have been written by medical authorities: *The Edgar Cayce Handbook for Health Through Drugless Therapy* (New York: 1975), by physiotherapist Dr. Harold J. Reilly and Ruth Hagy Brod, and *The Edgar Cayce Remedies* (New York: 1983) by William A. McGarey, MD. Dr. McGarey frequently prescribed Caster Oil pack for his patients, while using Glycothymoline packs for a host of problems: "Adhesions, arthritis, bronchitis, cataracts, catarrh (nasal), cold congestion, cystitis, cysts, epilepsy, eyes, glands, goiter, hay fever, migraine, herpes simplex, injuries, intestines, kidneys, lesions, paralysis, Parkinson's disease, pelvic disorders (over 40 cases), ptomaine poisoning, sciatica, sinusitis, subluxations, throat, tonsillitis, toxemia, tumors." According to Dr. Jim Harris, Edgar Cayce was way ahead of his times in his approach to healing:

> Central in Cayce's "psychic diagnoses" is the importance of balancing, harmonizing, and relaxing the entire system. Critical to this end are restoring proper elimination, and quieting inflammation and irritation.[8]

Not only did Edgar Cayce give medical clairvoyant advice, but he also instructed others on psychic development.

> As the entity studies, develops, and seeks, such application
> may be gained or attained by those forces thought which
> attunement is gained. As is seen all forms of vibration, whether
> in the mineral, in the vegetable, in the animal, in music, in
> those of chemics or chemicals, of those of spiritual vibration...
> (Reading 256-2)

In others words, if one seeks only the highest, that vibration of highest
good will come through.

Not only is medical clairvoyance popular in the United States,
but also in England, where Harry Edwards, Dr. Douglas Baker, and
George Chapman have worked. Harry Edwards did not diagnose as
Cayce's did; instead he focused on laying on of hands healings. When
the printer visited a Spiritualist meeting, he was told by the medium
that he would be good at spiritual healing. Almost immediately, he
was successful in his attempts at healing. For example, when a woman
was brought into Harry Edward's healing room in a wheel chair with
twisted hands and immobile feet, Edwards put the woman at ease
and took her hands.

> He put his hands on her knees and he worked them and it is
> as if his hands were going into the joints and massaging and
> loosening them. He was such a good healer.[9]

When the healing ended, the woman who had been wheeled into Harry
Edwards office walked out without the aid of even a walking stick! Edwards
died in 1976, just about the time Dr. Douglas Baker began Claregate
College, first in the United Sates in 1972, and later in England in 1977.
Dr. Baker encouraged hundreds in their esoteric studies in psychology,
astrology, occult chemistry, and the akashic records. Many of Dr. Baker's
books have been written with assistance from his spirit guide, Robert
Browning. In *Esoteric Healing, Part II*, Baker discusses the role of man's
seven bodies in relation to illness. Often illness, such as alcoholism, can
affect not only the physical body, but the etheric and astral bodies, as
well as the other finer bodies. For example, alcohol wreaks havoc on
body, mind, and spirit. According to Dr. Baker:

> The deadening of the body by alcohol to the effects of pain
> is the first indication that the etheric matrix is becoming
> "thinned out" if not actually detached from the physical body.
> Not only is diminishing judgment impairing the efficiency
> of the body functions but there is literally less vital energy
> being made available to the physical organs, the muscles,
> nerves, etc.[10]

Once the etheric body is deregulated, the astral body will also be effected. Scientists know that alcohol can limit REM or dream sleep which occurs when the astral body moves about during sleep. Soon the mental and other spiritual bodies are affected. That is why the alcoholic may lose all desire for life and turn to suicide. Dr. Baker observed:

> The suicide rate of alcoholics is extremely high and the astral world has a high percentage of its population made up of discarnate alcoholics. Their numbers are excessive because unlike other discarnate groups, their worldly desires are, in most instances, unrequited.[11]

Often, clairvoyants, such as C.W. Leadbeater, see these astral alcoholics haunting around bars, still craving alcohol with little awareness that they are dead! According to Dr. Baker, the effects of alcohol arouse both the third eye or Ajna chakra and the solar plexus which rules personal power. This would account for the hallucination alcoholics experience during the later stages of the disease. As Dr. Baker explained:

> These visual experiences result on the one hand from a wearing through of the etheric webs that separate the chakras from each other, thus giving the normal energies of the etheric spine a freer passage for their tidal flows upwards. On the other hand, the chakra in the brow becomes excessively stimulated by the alcohol on its own, whereas the safe process in Yoga is to open the three head centers simultaneously.[12]

Another excellent healer from the British Isles is medium George Chapman (1921-2006). For fifty years, Chapman has channeled the spirit of Dr. William Lang, free of charge, for those who needed his services. Writer, J. Bernard Hutton, who himself was saved from blindness, wrote a book in 1966, *Healing Hands*, which details Chapman's superb healing. According to Hutton:

> People who knew Dr. Lang in life reported that Chapman, in trance, perfectly captured Lang's personality and mannerisms; moreover, "Lang" recognized his former patients without an introduction, and knew things about them that only he and they could know.[14]

Dr. Lang's spirit healings which worked on the spirit body after he gently separated it from the physical form were nothing short of amazing. For instance, when Mrs. James was struck by an Aston Martin, she required extensive plastic surgery. Dr. Lang stepped in from the spirit world and did the plastic surgery so skillfully that there was no need for the physical plastic surgeon to operate. According to Mrs. James:

> ...with powder on you can't see a thing – and when the lady doctor from the Stoke Mandeville Hospital examined me, she was stunned. She couldn't understand it. She said there was no need for plastic surgery now.

Countless others have been headed by Dr. Lang through the mediumship of George Chapman, including a friend of Dr. John Best who was given only eight months to live due to a thyroid condition. Best details show after a few visits for contact healing by Dr. Lang, her terminal illness was cured, and she became active in life again.[16]

How did it feel to have an operation by Dr. Lang? Well Morton B. Jackson, a California lawyer described his operation for rheumatoid spondylitis, a painful condition that attacks both the joints and ligament, as follows:

> After a cordial conversation, Dr. Lang began his spirit operation on Jackson who became aware of the sharp cracking noise of his snapping fingers occasionally accompanied by instructions to Basil (Dr. Lang's son who died in 1928) and others apparently assisting him. The nature of the touch white light, seemed consistent with the handling and utilization of invisible instruments.[17]

George Chapman, while unusual in his ability, is not alone. There are many fine healers in England including Steven Upton, who teaches mediumship at the Arthur Findlay College in Stanstead, England As a trance medium, he works with spirit guide Dr. Joseph Lister. Upton points out:

> Trance healing involves three components: Spirit, a medium, and a patient. It is a passive process, as opposed to the active process of contact healing, allowing Spirit and the power of God's love direct access to the medium through whom specific healing energies are then directed to where ever needed in the patient. It is a very natural process which can affect the human form on many levels; physically, mentally, emotionally, and spiritually.[18]

Finally, Rev. Upton does not make any guarantee, and encourages his clients to use spirit healing as a complement to medical treatment.

Brazil has also produced some outstanding medical mediums – José Arigo and John of God. José Arigo (1921 –1971) was a Brazilian psychic surgeon who practiced in trance state with the spirit of Dr. Adolf Fritz doing the actual surgery. When he was fourteen, he met his spirit guide for the first time: According to his autobiography, around 1950, he began to suffer from strong headaches, insomnia, trances, and hallucinations. One day, he felt that the voice that had been pursuing him took over his body, and he had a vision of a bald man, dressed in a white apron and supervising a team of doctors and nurses in an enormous operating room. This entity identified itself as "Dr. Fritz." Soon Dr. Fritz began to work with the young medium. Eventually, his work attracted investigators such as Dr. Henry K. Puharich and author John G. Fuller who wrote *The Surgeon of a Rusty Knife* which tells Argo's story.

Another psychic surgeon, Rev. Alex Orbito, was featured in Shirley McLain's book, *Going Within*. Since then he has healed the sick in sixty countries, and has been researched by scientist, German physicist, and chemist, Alfred Stelter PhD; American biochemist, Dr. Donald G. Westerbeke; Dutch neurologist, Jan van Hemert PhD; Canadian, Dr. Lee Pulos PhD; and Japanese researcher, Dr. Kenzo Yamamoto.[19] How does Rev. Orbito heal? Basically, he goes into a trance state and his spirit guides perform real operations which include the removal of tumors, eye surgery, and even the removal of negative spirits. While his procedure may be viewed with a wary eye, a recent YouTube video shows what is termed a solar plexus cleaning. The video clearly shows Rev. Orbito placing his hands on the bare abdomen of an attractive blond woman. Within seconds his hand enter the body cavity and pulls out what looks like tissue. An assistant deftly wipes up the blood.[20] As for his critics, Rev. Orbito states: "My mission is not to convince, but to cure."[2]

Many consider another psychic surgeon, John of God, to be the greatest medical medium alive today. Born João Teixeira de Faria on June 24, 1942, he was unaware of his healing ability until he had a vision of Saint Rita of Cascia. She told the teenager that he was a healer and that she would always help him as long as he did not charge for healing. Other guides soon followed.

> Sometimes the spirits show up anonymously, but there are also several who make regular appearances. They include Dr. Augusto de Almeida, a surgeon and army man with a serious and efficient manner; Dr. Oswaldo Cruz, whose specialties were infectious diseases and bacteriology; Saint Francis Xavier, cofounder of the Jesuit Order, along with the Casa's patron, Saint Ignatius of Loyola, a priest and nobleman from the sixteenth century.[22]

These guides have healed people of cancers, AIDS, blindness, asthma, drug addiction, alcohol abuse, tumors, as well as autism and psychological problems.

Thousands visit his headquarters in Abadiania to pass before the medium. The spirit doctor prescribes treatment, which may take the form of herbs, pills, or even psychic surgery.

> When called for a surgical operation by João, patients are offered the choice of visible or invisible operations. If they select an invisible operation (or are younger than 18 or older than 45) they are directed to sit in a room in the Casa and meditate. João enters the room and pronounces "In the name of Jesus Christ you are all cured. Let what needs to be done be done in the name of God."[23]

Wisely, John of God tells people to continue taking their prescribed medication and the guides are not able to cure everyone. While John of God does not accept money for his healings, there is a small fee ($15-$36 in U.S. dollars) for the herbs which the entities prescribe.

In the United States, Caroline Myss (1952-) has done much to popularize medical intuition with her 1996 book, *Anatomy of the Spirit*. She was inspired by an interview with Dr. Elizabeth Kubler-Ross to pursue a Master's Degree in theology which she obtained from Mundelein College in Chicago in 1979. A few years later, in 1982, Myss started giving medical intuitive readings which led to her collaboration with Dr. Norman Shealy. When her book, *Anatomy of Spirit* was published in 1996, Myss became nationally known for her work on energy healing according to the Hindu chakra system in the body. According to Myss:

> Intuition is a natural by-product of flowering of a mature self-esteem and a sense of empowerment – not power over, but power to be.[24]

Scanning the Body

Most people, with a little practice, are able to pick up the energy field of the body. Choose a partner to practice on. First, with one hand, make a slow sweep of the body of your partner. Begin at the top of the head and criss-cross deliberately down the body to the feet. Note any hot or cold spots and when you finish, ask the person if there is any significance to the hot and cold areas. Often they will be places which have imbalances either in the past or present. For example, a sluggish thyroid, heart condition, a back ache, or even an old fracture may register as a hot or cold spot. Share the information with your partner. Ask for feedback. Then switch and allow your partner to scan you. Please keep in mind that you are not a doctor and cannot diagnose. Simply describe what you are "feeling."

End Notes

1. www.ppquimby.com.
2. www.ppquimby.com.
3. www.ppquimby.com.
4. www.andrewjacksondavis.com/.
5. www.andrewjacksondavis.com/.
6. www.andrewjacksondavis.com/.
7. Andrew Jackson Davis, *Principles of Nature* (1847) page 62.
8. Dr. Harold Reilly EC Drugless..p. 359 http://home.earthlink.net/~jimrharris/tecr.html.
9. http://home.earthlink.net/~jimrharris/tecr.html.
10. http://www.spiritualistresources.com/cgi-bin/healing/index.pl?read=5".
11. http://members.fortunecity.com/biugung1/alchoholism.html.
12. http://members.fortunecity.com/biugung1/alchoholism.html.
13. http://members.fortunecity.com/biugung1/alchoholism.html.
14. *Healing Hands,* 1978 revised edition, pages 64-68.
15. *Healing Hands,* 1978 revised edition, pages 64-68.
16. *Healing Hands,* 1978 revised edition, pages 64-68.
17. *Psychic World,* July 1993.
18. G.Chapman, Ibid, 41,42(15) Cit. http://en.wikipedia.org/wiki/Z%C3%A9_Arig%C3%B3.
19. http://www.auragraphs.com/index.php?act=viewDoc&docId=5.
20. http://www.pyramidofasia.org/.
21. MiraMahoneyhttp://gdata.you tube.com/feeds/api/users/miramohoneyEducation SolarPlexusChakraClearing Psychic Surgery-Rev. Alex Orbito in Phillipines.
22. http://www.pyramidofasia.org/22 John of God 23 john of God 24 Myss.
23. http://www.oprah.com/spirit/Spiritual-Healer-John-of-God-Susan-Casey/4.
24. http://en.wikipedia.org/wiki/Jo%C3%A3o_de_Deus_(medium).

Suggested Reading

Rev. Andrew Jackson Davis. *Principles of Nature*
John DeSalvo. *Andrew Jackson Davis*
Caroline Myss. *Anatomy of Spirit*
Dr. Harold Reilly. *Edgar Cayce Drugless Healing*
Dr. Norman Shealy. *Medical Intuition*

Fourteen

Electronic Mediumship

When working with etheric energy, the expectation of the practitioner/ witness defines the experience.

~Association TransCommunication

Today, mediumship can take many forms. While some mediums concentrate their efforts on healing, others focus on psychic photography and electronic voice phenomena. The best thing about electronic mediumship is you do not have to be a clairvoyant or even a medium to prove the continuity of life. All you need is the right equipment, some technique, and a little patience.

Ghost hunters, Grant Wilson and Jason Hawes, routinely use various electronic equipment, which they believe is capable of detecting paranormal activity on their Syfy television program. The two plumbers began *Ghost Hunters* in 1996. One of the reasons that the show is so successful, is the emphasis on research. The Atlantic Paranormal Society, or TAPS, is careful to choose sites that have valid histories of paranormal activity. According to Grant Wilson, it is important to start the investigation with a clean slate:

> If you are simply ghost hunting, you need to do research in order to know where to go and when. But if you are on an investigation, then you need to do your research afterwards.[1]

He also advises investigators to log every event and detail for later study.

When called in on a case, they try to first find reasonable explanation for the haunting. For instance, cold spots could be paranormal activity or drafty windows. The same for orbs, which could just be dust particles. As for phantom lights, they would have to rule out things as the reflection of lights from other sources, such as mirrors or even passing cars. Ectoplasm could be smoke from a cigarette. TAPS, by the way, has a strict *no smoking* policy for that very reason.

As for catching genuine spirits on film, Grant Wilson advises the researcher to try to surprise the ghosts, as not all wish to be photographed:

> Some ghosts want to be caught on film, some don't care, others don't want to be caught at all. Because we don't know the ghost's feelings about this, there is only one way to pretty much guarantee that you'll catch it on film. This is by casually snapping a picture, over your shoulder even, whenever you get the inkling to.[2]

Often, the ghost hunters will have an overnight stakeout with a video camera to capture orb spirit lights, or objects that move on their own. They also use digital recorders to capture the sound of spirit footsteps or even the voices of the deceased through electronic voice phenomena. Ron Milione advises:

> Human-sounding voices from unknown origin are recorded on such electronic media as tape recorders, digital voice recorders, video recorders, and other devices. Strangely, the voices are not heard at the time of the recording; it is only when the recording is played back that the voices are heard.[3]

TAPS charges no fee, not even expenses for their service and is willing to travel to places like the Derby's Sterling Opera House. Built in 1889, the building has been used as a city hall, police station, and a jail. Amy Bruni, a member of the Ghost Hunters team explains why the team chose the Sterling Opera House:

> The building has been undergoing renovations, and those who have been inside say they've seen things they can't quite explain.[4]

What did Jason and Grant uncover? During the "The Reveal" with Rich DiCarlo, they show him footage of Dave and Tango reacting to the sound of a bang in the theater that was heard after Tango's magic tricks as well as several EVPs:

> ...one that sounds like a kid's voice that Jason and Grant record in the balcony (while the K2 is lit up); a "moan" that Grant and Jason captured in the dressing room; and another "groan" that Amy and Adam record during an EVP session.[5]

Gaining rapport with spirit with magic tricks or simple coaxing is a vital part of ghost hunting. For example, Jason Hawes used psychology to coax the spirit of a little girl who died in a old New Hampshire inn. He talked to the spirit child about being a dad to his five children in order to engage a young girl who had died in the very room in which he was sitting. It is important to note he addressed the spirit child by name and spoke directly to her as if she was in the room.

When it comes to ghost hunting psychology, it is just as important as equipment. Ghost anthropologist John G. Sabol, author of *Gettysburg Unearthed*, would agree. He also likes to coax the spirits a bit. At one haunted location where the spirit of a Union soldier had been sighted in Gettysburg, he even hired a prostitute to "tease" the spirit out! While most ghost hunters are content to use psychic photography to capture ghostly orbs, Sabol examines the infrastructure from the bottom up. This ghost excavator with a Masters in Anthropology begins with an onsite investigation which includes many layers of history, followed by careful evaluation of the data, including videos that are recorded at haunted locations.

Amateur ghost hunters can also capture spirit on videos and film with some simple steps:

Rule One: For psychic photography: Choose your location carefully. Do the research. What places in your area are known to be haunted? Perhaps a neighbor has heard footsteps at night when no one else is home. Another choice would be an historic site such as Gettysburg. Some ghost hunters, such as John Zaffis, have had success in cemeteries. Zaffis tells the story of how one night, when he was returning from a paranormal investigation with his aunt and uncle, ghost hunters, Ed and Lorrain Warren, he saw a lady in white walking through Union Cemetery in Easton, Connecticut. All three clearly saw the apparition, but alas no one had a camera!

Rule Two: Be prepared with a camera, preferably a digital with at least eight pixels and extra batteries as spirit can easily drain the energy. When the author visited Lily Dale Assembly in New York with four students, all five of our cameras went dead after a brief evening photo shoot outside the Lily Dale Museum. Fortunately, we had extra batteries and a few "throw away cameras" as back up.

Rule Three: Begin your photo shoot with a prayer of intention. Ask the spirits' permission to take their photos. Be clear in your intent. For instance, "Hello, we are interested to showing spirit activity. If spirits are present, please show yourselves." If you are psychic you may feel a chill down your spine or see a flash of light. For those without psychic abilities, use an EMF meter to locate electromagnetic energy which may indicate spirit.

Rule Four: When you are ready to take the photograph, point your camera in that area. Don't be concerned that you cannot see any ghostly activity. Most people do not see orbs or mists until they look at the finished picture. By the way, if you are shooting at night, or in dark area, you will probably need to use a flash, unless you are using an infrared camera. With practice and patience, most ghost hunters will be rewarded with some of the following psychic images:

Orbs – Transparent round spheres that may occasionally have a face appear in the middle of them.

Ghost Lights – A steak of light; sometimes it will have a distinct color.

Light Rod – A stick which sometimes will swirl or bend in shape.

Vortex – Funnel shape which can sometimes be seen moving on video camera.

Ectoplasm – A fog or mist often in strategic areas. Physical mediums can produce enough ectoplasm to materialize faces or figures.

Psychic photography is not an exact science, so take time to analyze your "psychic" images. It is easy to mistake rain drops or dust particles for orbs. Sometimes a lack of pixilation due to low light may also produce orbs. As for vortexes, Dale Kaczmarek, author of *Windy City Ghosts*, suggests:

> The great majority of vortex pictures are nothing more than accidentally photographing one's camera strap.[6]

Take care, then, to secure your camera strap so it is not dangling freely.

This is not to say that all "psychic photographs" are false positives. Many are genuine photos of spirit. In fact, some of the best have been taken at séances, notably those of Ethel Post Parrish, one of the most famous of materialization mediums of all times. While she was in trance, her guide, Silver Belle, materialized as well as spirits of loved ones known to the audience. At one of her séances:

> Ella Carter and a Dr. Baker, both in spirit, materialized for Joseph Graham, Bryn Mawr, Pennsylvania. These two held

the floor simultaneously and for several minutes talked to Mr. Graham.[9]

Fortunately, Ethel Post Parrish allowed psychic photographer Jack Edwards to take several pictures of Silver Belle materializing in front of eighty-one people during a 1953 séance. Edwards took pictures every fifty seconds using infrared film and obtained amazing results.

If you plan to take pictures during a séance, do not take a photograph while the medium is in trance, as the flash can jar both spirit and the medium! Sometimes a picture can be obtained if you ask permission beforehand. If possible, use an infra-red camera or turn off the flash on a regular camera, so as not to disturb the medium. Be patient. Remember also to be clear in your intention and ask spirit permission before you enter their realm. Don't forget to surround yourself with white light and a prayer for protection.

Another rare séance phenomena is skotography.

> This is a form of physical phenomena where Spirit Communication arrives via an instrument outside of the human medium's body. In this case the medium is photographic paper.[10]

This form of psychic photography requires a physical medium with the right body chemistry. In 1993, two couples, Robin and Sandy Foy and Diane and Alan Bennett sat for physical mediumship. During their 500 sittings in the basement of a home in Scole, England, the group had some interesting results with photography:

> Images were imprinted on unopened rolls of film inside a locked box. These images included actual photos of people and places, sometimes from the past, and various obscure verses and drawings that took some effort to identify. There were also pictures of other dimensions and the beings that inhabit them.[11]

Their efforts were chronicled in the book by Grant Solomon, *The Scole Experiment*, which was released in 2000. Not only can spirit be captured on film, but on recorders as well. Capturing the voice of spirit is just as evidential as capturing orbs or spirit outlines. This phenomena known as Electronic Voice Phenomena (EVP) was discovered by Dr. Constantine Raudive. According to lawyer-turned-psychic researcher Victor Zammit:

> For more than fifty years, experimenters all over the world have been tape recording "paranormal voices" – voices which cannot

be heard when a tape recorder is playing but which can be heard when the tape is played back. Many of the very short messages claim to be from loved ones who have passed on.[12]

Sadly, many EVPs go unnoticed on tape because often EVPs are not heard during the recording but will be heard faintly on the playback, especially if head phones and amplification are used. Occasionally, spirit voices are recorded in reverse. The voices when they are being recorded are not heard to the experimenter at the time of the experiment and only discerned when the tape is played back. Sometimes spirit voices will be recorded in reverse, while other times they will answer questions or even call the experimenter by name.

If you wish to try your hand at EVPs, find a location that may have some paranormal activity such as the home of the deceased or places where spirit has been spotted. You will need a tape or digital recorder and some form of white noise is needed for the spirit to create sounds. Use the sound of a hair dryer or even running water. Then say a prayer of protection. Next, try to gain rapport by talking to the spirits. Often this takes a few preliminary questions such as, "Who is here?" Then wait thirty seconds. Next, you could ask permission to tape them. Wait thirty seconds. You might ask if spirit has a message. Again wait, and then announce you are closing the session and ask any last-minute messages. Then wait a moment before you close the session.

With some patience and practice, most researchers can master the art of recording EVPs, especially with a digital tape recorder which can be linked directly to the computer to amplify sound. Afterwards, you can obtain a voice graph with computer software such as *Audition* or an *Audacity* sound editor which can amplify, filter, and even reverse sound file. According to Tom Butler:

> You can either make the recording on a tape recorder and then play the tape into the computer for review, editing, and storage, or attach a microphone directly to the computer and use the sound editor as a tape recorder.[13]

Once you have your watch graph on the computer, tune into the valleys between the sound peaks, as EVPs will often come between the human voices. Also be sure to use amplification and ear phones to clearly hear the spirit voices which are often inaudible to the naked ear.

Sometimes, a group effort will speed things along, as Robin and Sandy Foy and Diane and Alan Bennett found out when they tried their hand at EVP. Their efforts were richly awarded with an EVP recording which included an audible performance of Rachmaninoff's Second Concerto. What was the key to their phenomenal success? Their spirit

An angel in the fire. This angel appeared during a fire ceremony. Notice the picture is an upside-down photograph of the camp fire! *Photographer: Elaine M. Kuzmeskus*

guide, Manu, came through to advise them on electronic mediumship which included EVP recordings of spirit voices which could be heard by everyone in the room!

End Notes

1. www.the-atlantic-paranormal-society.com/articles/general/research. html.
2. www.the-atlantic-paranormal-society.com/articles/general/proof1. html.
3. www.the-atlantic-paranormal-society.com/articles/technical/ whitenoise.html.
4. www.wtnh.com/dpp/news/new_haven_cty/ghost-hunters-tv-show-in-derby.
5. www.damnedct.com/ghost-hunters-sterling-opera-house./
6. www.ghostresearch.org/.
7. www.answers.com/topic/john-myers.
8. Christopher Balzano, *Picture Yourself Capturing Ghosts on Film*, Course Technology, 2009, page 85.
9. Jay Strong, "Ethel Post-Parrish Carried From The Cabinet While In Trance."
10. www.victorzammit.com/book/chapter04.html+EVP+ COnstantine+Raudive.
11. http://zohrala.com/mediums/class/skotography.htm.
12. http://atransc.org/techniques.htmgive.
13. http://atransc.org/techniques.htmgive.

Suggested Reading

Christopher Balzano. *Picture Yourself Capturing Ghosts on Film*
Clement Cheroux. *The Perfect Medium: Photography and the Occult*
Jim Eaton. *Ghosts Caught on Film II*
Fred Gettings. *Ghosts in Photographs*
John Harvey. *Photography and Spirit*
Martyn Jolly. *Faces of the Living Dead*
Dale D. Kaczmarek. *A Field Guide to Spirit Photography*
Louis Kaplan. *The Strange Case of William Mumler*
Elaine Kuzmeskus. *Séance 101*
Leonore Sweet. *How to Photograph the Paranormal*
Melvin Willin. *Ghosts Caught on Film*

Fifteen

Table Tipping, Levitation, Spoon-Bending, and Apports

You cannot separate creative and psychic ability.

~Seth

Table Tipping

Today's enthusiasm for electronic mediumship today is similar to the Victorian craze for table tipping. In this type of séance, sitters place their hands on a round table and wait for contact. Spiritualism began with raps and table tipping of the Fox Sisters in 1848. By 1853, the movement and the practice of table tipping had spread to England where it quickly became an acceptable method of contacting the spirit world.

The method was simple enough. Several people sat around the table with their hands resting on it and waited patiently for the spirit to communicate. If the table rotated back and forth, contact was assumed made. Then the table would communicate by tilting as the appropriate letter was voiced, thus spelling out words and sentences. While French Spiritist, Allan Kardec attributed the movement to invisible spirit hands, others such as Dr. John Elliotson and his followers attributed the phenomena to mesmerism. The general public were content to find the explanation of the movements in spirits, animal magnetism, odic force, galvanism, electricity, or even the rotation of the earth.[1]

The Scottish surgeon and hypnotist, James Braid, wisely noted that the success of table tipping was increased by suggestion given to sitters and their expectations. Thus, positive suggestion and expectation seem part of the explanation for table tipping which is still being used as a means of communicating with the other side. When choosing a table, start with a small wooden three-legged table, about thirty inches in height. Next, cleanse it. This can easily be done by lightly spraying salt water on the table. If you do not live near the ocean, a solution of sea salt and a quart of water will do the trick. Place a half of cup of sea salt (not table salt) in a spray bottle with a quart of water. Gently spray it on the table. As you wipe the water off, send the thought that you are clearing the table of negativity.

Next, call on your guides and dedicate the table to spiritual use with a prayer and an affirmation such as, "This table is cleansed and dedicated to Spirit." Now you are ready to invite like-minded friends to join you in table tipping. Usually three to six people work best depending on the size of the table. In any event, it is important for the group to be willing to meet regularly, as it may take time to connect with spirit. When you do, you will wish to keep a record of the messages received with a tape recorder. Also, place a glass of water nearby for sitters. Water facilitates spirit communication. If you wish you may use crystals and incense to increase the psychic energy in the room. Also, turn off the ringer on the telephone.

Now you are ready to begin. Start your table tipping with a prayer. Then have each member of the group place his or her fingers and palms down lightly on the table. Some mediums like the thumb of one participant to touch the little finger of the next for an unbroken circle. By the way, table tipping does not require a dark room, and can be easily be done in daylight. Then the group should sing some songs to raise the vibration. Standards such as "Row, Row, Row Your Boat" or "You Are My Sunshine" work nicely. With regular practice, your fingers will begin to feel sticky as if they are melding into the table. This is a sure sign that you are making progress. Soon the table should vibrate a bit. Try sending energy from one sitter to another across the table. At first the table will move little bit. With practice, it will move back and forth.

Often sitters like to establish a code at this point. A code such as moving can mean *yes*, and *no* could be no movement. If you wish, you could also try a code for *yes* – moving to the back of the room and *no* moving to the front of the room. At first you will need to confine yourself to *yes* and *no* questions. Later, try working with the alphabet: one movement for *A*, two for *B*, and so on. It is not unusual for a three-legged table to get up on one leg or even spin around on its own. Some table tippers have even gotten the table to levitate off the ground a few inches. It may even walk down the room on its own volition, with the medium just placing one hand on it. At one séance at the author's home, the table moved across the living room and turned a corner, went down a hall, and stopped in front of her office door.

Levitation

Not only tables can levitate, but people from yogis to mediums also have been seen levitating. Sometimes, this happens spontaneously as in the case of saints and yogis, such as Subbayah Pullavar, have conscious control of the process. Yogi Pullavar, also known as Subbayah Pullavar, was an Indian man who, on June 6, 1936, was reported to have levitated into the air for four minutes in front of a crowd of 150 witnesses. According to *TIME* magazine:

> Subbayah crawled in between the tent supports, lay down beside
> a draped stick set up in the ground. At the base of the stick he
> seated, with much show of tenderness, a malevolent-looking
> little doll. A helper hung cloth tent-walls around Subbayah. Few
> minutes later the walls were stripped away. There was Subbayah,
> hanging shelf-like to the top of the draped stick.[2]

The phenomenon is not confined to yogis. While levitation is quite rare among mediums, it has been documented, notably in the cases of Daniel Douglas Home and Colin Evans. Daniel Douglas Home, a physical medium, was seen rising five to seven feet above the ground: Home's fame grew, fuelled by his ostensible feats of levitation. William Crookes claimed to know of more than fifty occasions in which Home levitated "in good light" (gas light) at least five to seven feet above the floor. Home's feats were recorded by Frank Podmore:

> We all saw him rise from the ground slowly to a height of about
> six inches, remain there for about ten seconds, and then slowly
> descend.[3]

Another famous physical medium known for his levitation was of Colin Evans. During a 1938 séance, Evans was captured levitating above the audience. The picture,[4] taken in infra-red light, shows Evans with his eyes closed and an intense look of concentration on his face as he remained in the air for some time. Apparently it requires a great amount of concentration to the depth of trance needed for levitation.

While scientific experiments involving levitation are rare, science has conducted some. Parapsychology labs such as the Rhine Research Center at Duke University regularly test for what is termed PK or psychokinesis. For the past seventy years, the Rhine Center has taken measurements of psi (pounds per square inch) by looking at the physiological changes or bioenergy characteristics of psychics. In the Soviet Union, Nina Kulagina (1926-1990) has been photographed levitating a small object between her hands.

Nina said that in order to manifest the effect, she required a period of meditation to clear her mind of all thoughts. When she had obtained the focus required, she reported a sharp pain in her spine and the blurring of her eyesight.[4]

Unfortunately, the PK medium suffered a heart attack in the late 1970s and had to limit her PK experiments thereafter.

Spoon-Bending

Bending spoons is fast becoming a popular form of psychokinesis. Ron Nagy who teaches a course on the subject feels that most people can learn to bend spoons using the power of their mind if they are willing to let go of limiting beliefs:

> During our lives we have programmed ourselves with many negative thought patterns that block higher energies that empower us. One must learn how to let go of all former limitations... "To let go and let God."[5]

During his workshop, participants are encouraged to maintain a light atmosphere to lift the vibration. Then, at the right moment, each person concentrates and then let's go. With practice, most people are able to bend their silver-plated or stainless-steel spoons by the end of the workshop. Some, such as Ronald Kuzmeskus, not only bent his spoon, but twisted it into curls.

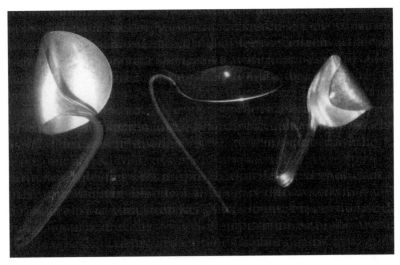

Three spoons bent by Ronald Kuzmeskus at a workshop given by Ron Nagy

Apports

While the average person can learn to bend spoons, only a few gifted mediums can produce apports. It is even rarer than levitation. However, during the heydays of Spiritualism, the production of apports was one of the features of Spiritualistic séances. Apports are usually small objects, such as flowers or jewelry, and literally appeared out of nowhere and dropped into the laps of the sitters or flew through trumpets onto the floor. Spiritualists believe that apports are brought into the séance room by spirits:

> Most apports are considered gifts from spirits, but some mediums claim to pull objects from other dimensions, or that objects existing in other places are disintegrated, transported by the medium into the medium's location, and then reassembled – all by the power of the medium's psyche.[6]

Of course, not all apports came directly from the spirit world; some were smuggled into the séance room by unscrupulous mediums who concealed the apports about their person. Even though the number of apport séances have decreased in recent years with the increase in the number of exposed mediums, that does not mean that some apports are not genuine.

For instance, Rev. Kenneth Custance was in a séance room in Chesterfield, Indiana, when a gentleman received a black onyx "knight's ring." He excitedly said, "This is the ring I lost in California." Rev. Custance was skeptical that the stone had been materialized from his California home to Camp Chesterfield. He said to the California sitter, "How could you possibly tell one black onyx ring from another?" The ring's owner, carefully showed the minister, a chip in the left-hand corner. "See that chip? I noticed it when planning to have the ring reset the day I lost it."

Rev. Kenneth Custance gave another account of unexpected apports received by author Faith Baldwin on her birthday. Shortly after the death of her beloved husband, Faith placed a fresh flower by her husband's picture. One day as she emptied the vase, beautiful Persian gemstones fell out. She quickly fished them out of the sink and brought the rare stones to her New York jeweler to set in a bracelet. When the surprised jeweler saw the stones, he asked how she obtained perfectly-matched Persian gems, Faith answer,ed "With great difficulty!"

Another account of apport phenomena which rings true is found in Doreen Phillips' book, *Autobiography of a Fortune Teller.* The clairvoyant spent several weeks studying at Camp Chesterfield in Indiana, and on her last day, she was rewarded with a very evidential apport during a séance with Rev. Lillian Dee Johnson at Camp Chesterfield:

> ...in this class on apports, it was explained the object first had
> to be dematerialized and then rematerialized, and that when
> we received it, it was often warm. We were asked not to press
> it until it set. [6]

Naturally she was thrilled when she received a beautiful large jade scarab just as her spirit guide had promised. It was even more authentic because it had an Arabic inscription on the back. When Phillips did some research, she found out that Masudi was an Arabic scholar who wrote *Meadows of Gold and Mine of Gems* in 932! [8]

While Rev. Johnson's séance took place in the 1950s, more recently, Scole Experiment Group has had success in the production of apports. Their amazing apports included a Churchill coin, silver necklace, silver bracelet, and an original fresh copy of *Daily Mail* 1/4/44, On the evening the *Daily Mail* newspaper was approved, the late medium Helen Duncan was present to wish the sitter good luck.

> After that session, the group discovered that the new apport was a
> mint copy of *The Daily Mail*, dated Saturday, 1/4/44, which showed
> Helen Duncan's "guilty" verdict at the infamous trial.[9]

End Notes

1. *Modern Practical Guide to Table Tilting* (from ASSAP) based on the work of Ken Batcheldor Museum of Talking Boards.
2. www.time.com/time/magazine/article/0,9171,770234-2,00.html.
3. en.wikipedia.org/wiki/Daniel_Dunglas_Home.
4. www.fun-on.com/science_nina_kulagina_telekinesis.php.
5. ronnagy.net/ronsblog/spoon-bending/.
6. www.answers.com/topic/apports.
7. Doreen Phillips' book, *Autobiography of a Fortune Teller*, Vantage Press, New York, NY 1958, page 82.
8. Doreen Phillips' book, *Autobiography of a Fortune Teller*, Vantage Press, New York, NY 1958, page 83.
9. http://www.victorzammit.com/articles/scole2.

Suggested Reading

Nandor. *Between Two Worlds*
Rosemary Ellen Guiley. *The Encyclopedia of Ghosts and Spirits*
Doreen Phillips. *Autobiography of a Fortune Teller*
Charles Richet. *Thirty Years of Psychical Research*
Walter and Mary Jo Uphoff. *New Psychic Frontiers*
J.C.F. Zollner. *Transcendental Physics*

Sixteen

Channeling

Under all circumstances, keep an even mind.

~Rev. Andrew Jackson Davis

In order to obtain the powers of a medium, such as Rev. Lillian Dee Johnson, or those in the Scole Group, it is necessary to become a channeler or what used to be called a trance medium. What constitutes "trance mediumship?" There are many ways of measuring trance states. While old time Spiritualists might stick a pin into a medium's arm to check trance, science may measure today's channelers' brain waves with an electroencephalograph. The lower the frequency of cycles per second (cps) known as Hertz (Hz), the more your awareness is turned inward and relaxed.

Brainwave Frequency	State of Consciousness	Cycles Per Second (cps)
Beta	Relaxed, "zoned out"	14 - 40 cps
Alpha	Relaxed, light trance	8 - 13 cps
Theta	Deeply Relaxed, deeper trance	4 - 7 cps
Delta	Dreamless, full trance	0.5 - 3.5 cps

While a mental medium operates in the Alpha state, a trance medium would be in the Theta to Delta brain frequency. Most channelers usually operate in the Theta trance with some conscious awareness, but only a few are full trance mediums in the Delta state of consciousness. In addition to the level of trance, there is a shift in spirit communication with each phase of mediumship. Mental mediumship has spirit using the medium's mind to communicate mind to mind, whereas in trance mediumship, spirit overshadows the medium as in light trance and may actually take over the medium's body in full trance. This is done with the medium's permission, as opposed to possession where spirits use the medium's mind without consent. Castillo explains:

> Trance phenomena result from the behavior of intense focusing of attention, which is the key psychological mechanism of trance induction. Adaptive responses, including institutionalized forms of trance, are "tuned" into neural networks in the brain.[1]

In channeling, which is also known as deep trance or "dead" trance, the medium loses all consciousness of what is said during the session. These full trance mediums were quite popular in the 1860s and 1870s at Lily Dale Assembly in New York and other Spiritualist camps; trance mediums gave passionate speeches on the issues of the day such as temperance, marriage, and women's suffrage. In America (1857-1950), Leonora Piper was considered by many to be the most famous trance medium of her day.

Most mediums are in a light state of trance when they connect with spirit. However, as they progress, they often wish to deepen the connection with the other world through a deeper trance. How can this be accomplished? According to Edgar Cayce, "Mind is the builder." He often pointed out the mind is the bridge between the physical world and the spiritual plane.

Hypnosis, which both Edgar Cayce and Andrew Jackson Davis used as a means to induce trance, can facilitate the powers of the mind, as well as spirit communication. Hypnosis has had an honorable history dating back to ancient Egypt and India. The Egyptians often used magic and hypnosis in their rituals, and the Hindus excelled in their knowledge of hypnosis, magic, and psychic powers.

One of the first hypnotists to rediscover the mystical aspects of hypnosis was Frenchman Charles Poyen. In 1836, he came to the United States to lecture on magnetism. *The Boston Medical and Surgical Journal* was sufficiently impressed by his demonstration of the anesthetic properties of hypnosis to carry a description of the procedure in its July edition. Later, Charles Poyen gained fame when his subject, Miss Cynthia Gleason, an English weaver, turned out to be a gifted clairvoyant under magnetism:

> Usually she made her diagnosis, passing her hand over the patient's body, head downward, describing as she did so, the various organs. She claimed the body became transparent and she could see the organs in detail. Often she described them in her homespun terms, pointing out visible signs of some disorder – white spots on the liver, pimples on the stomach, a spleen double its normal size. Miss Gleason was even able to

diagnose a person at a distance by just holding a lock of their hair.[1]

Often, the old time mediums referred to this type of clairvoyance as traveling clairvoyance. Today, it is known as remote viewing. A modern example of extraordinary clairvoyance and mediumship was demonstrated by Eileen Garret two days after the huge British airship, the *R101*, had crashed in France on October 5, 1930. When the dirigible went down, 48 of the 54 passengers were killed. A few days later, Eileen Garret was called in to do a séance to contact Sir Arthur Conan Doyle. Instead of reaching Conan Doyle, the voice of the flight commander of the *R101*, Flight Lieutenant H. Carmichael Irwin, came through with these pertinent details on the tragic crash. In anguished tones, the voice said:

> I must do something about it ... The whole bulk of the dirigible was entirely and absolutely too much for her engines' capacity. Engines too heavy. It was this that made me on five occasions have to scuttle to safety. Useful lift too small.[2]

Later a very thorough intelligence investigation validated Lieutenant Irwin's communication from beyond, when it disclosed that the *R101*'s heavy diesel engines were in part responsible for the deadly crash.

How did the Irish medium make such extraordinary contact with Irwin? There are two answers. One, Mrs. Garrett was a deep trance medium; and, two, her guides were able to facilitate the communication. Eileen J. Garrett (1893–1970) medium, author, and founder of the Parapsychology Foundation in New York City, believed in scientific study of paranormal phenomena . She trained in London to be a full trance medium. As a medium she attracted four highly evolved spirit guides:

> Garrett had four trance controls; Uvani, a fourteenth-century Arab soldier, was in primary control of her mediumship. Abdul Latif, a seventeenth-century Persian physician, dealt primarily with healing and would often cause her to speak in unknown dialects. Very seldom, she was contacted by the two final spirits who spoke only on spiritual matters, Tahotah and Ramah were their names, they claimed no earthy incarnations however several other mediums felt that they had a Native American connection.[3]

Guides are the essential component in mediumship and even more so for a trance medium, who must have complete confidence in their spirit control to allow the guide to take over. To reach higher levels of mediumship, a medium must deepen his or her trance state. Guides have a way of gradually taking over the medium. At first, spirit will stand behind the medium. Then with practice the guide will blend with the aura of the medium more and more until the guide overshadows the medium. This is the most common level of trance. The medium is conscious, but also aware spirit is talking through him. Many times mediums will say, "I don't remember the session." Only vaguely can they supply details. That is why it is a good idea to tape the reading. In the final stage, the medium will leave their body and the guide will enter. This takes not only permission of the medium, but also a very deep level of trance. Only a few mediums reach this level where they allow their guide to fully incorporate into their body. It takes many years to develop dead trance which is the strongest level of control.

While some trance mediums develop their gift through the use of hypnosis, others do so in a Spiritualist circle, and still others work on their own. Edgar Cayce, for instance, realized his deep trance mediumship when he was hypnotized by Al Layne to relieve hysterical paralysis of the vocal cords. Soon he learned to put himself into trance through self hypnosis. When in this deep state, he said he felt himself follow a pinpoint of light. While Cayce was astral traveling, the Source came in to answer questions posed by his secretary, Gladys Davis.

Today, mediumship students can go to places like the Arthur Findlay College in Stanstead, England, for trance instruction. The college is housed in a Tudor mansion which was once the home of Scottish stockbroker and Spiritualist, Arthur Findlay. It is surrounded by acres of manicured lawns, and its summer gardens are lush with flowers. Inside the walls of stately brick building are large rooms tastefully decorated with oil paintings of British aristocrats, oriental rugs, and priceless antiques.

Here, veteran mediums, Muriel Tennant, and Maureen Murman conduct week-long seminars on "The Journey of Trance." Each tutor takes a group of twelve students. At first, the students meditate in a group as the medium tunes into their energy. Once the aura of group members is harmoniously blended, the students are ready to link with spirit. Initially, they are told to relax. Next, the students are told to be receptive to spirit. As Muriel Tenant explained: "Allow spirit to contact you."

Muriel Tenant is one of the finest tutors at Arthur Findlay College. However, she did not start out to be a medium. The fashionably dressed expert was once the owner of a dress shop that turned out to be haunted. The ghost of the dress caused her to seek out assistance from the local Spiritualist church in the 1960s. Soon Tenant was in a development circle learning to communicate with the other side. This experience lead her to Spiritualism. Over the years, she honed her skill as a trance medium and a tutor at the Arthur Findlay College for the "Journey of Trance."

How did the group develop trance? It really was a gradual process of letting go which takes place over a week of training. At first, students are taught to relax and be receptive to spirit, while the tutor monitors the auras of the group. Then the students work in groups of four. The group meditates in front of the other eight students who describe the spirit activity around the trance students. By the end of six days, each group picks their best trance student for talent night.

In the United States, Camp Chesterfield offers trance training with mediums Rev. Suzanne Greer, Rev. Patricia Kennedy, and Rev. Glenda (Freeman) Cadarella. When the author visited the camp in January 2012, she had a private reading with Glenda who gave her names of her guides – Bright Star, Dr. Englewood, and Clifford Bias with his black panther. Later that evening, during the "Guides and Loved Ones Séance," Dr. Buchanan, the medium's guide, announced: "Elwood is here for three of you." This turned out to be true as I was there with two others from our Cabinet Group which is often guided by Elwood Babbitt.

Then Glenda channeled Ashtar, who told the group: "You have agreed to be here for the awakening and you cannot turn back." Master Ashtar also stated there would be weather changes for two generations and eventually our DNA structure would change. While it took many years for Glenda Cadarella to develop deep trance channeling, most students can achieve a light state of trance through hypnosis. Here is an exercise to assist you on your journey of trance.

Hypnosis Exercise: Progressive Relaxation

Try this hypnosis exercise to relax your body. For best results have someone read it to you.

First, sit in a comfortable position, sitting in a chair or lying on a couch. Do not cross your legs or arms.

Now take a deep breath through the nose and out through the mouth. Do this three times.

Relax your eyes. Visualize white lotus blossoms serenely floating in a pool of aqua water. See your eyes as beautiful lotus blossoms completely tranquil.

Let this feeling of relaxation go into your forehead, erasing all cares. Then gently into the cheeks, chin and throat. All tension is released in the throat.

Allow this relaxation to flow into the shoulders, releasing all pressure in the muscles.

Now visualize this relaxation going down your right shoulder to your right elbow to your right wrist to your right hand. Completely relax.

Elwood Babbitt, Premiere Trance Medium

Let this relaxation flow into your left shoulder, down your left arm to your left elbow to your left wrist, so your whole left arm is completely relaxed.

Feel this gentle relaxation flow down your spine, so your spine is as limp and flexible as a piece of spaghetti.

Your shoulder, spine, and back are completely relaxed. Your chest is relaxed. All tension is released from your shoulders, chest, lungs, heart, and stomach.

All organs are operating smoothly, effortlessly.

This relaxation goes into your hips. Down the right hip to the right knee to the right ankle, so your whole right leg is relaxed.

Feel this gentle relaxation flow down your left leg to your left knee to your left ankle, so your whole left leg is relaxed.

Your whole body is now relaxed from the top of your head to the soles of your feet.

Take a moment to tune into the other side of life.

Allow your loved ones, guides, and angels to speak to you now.

Play new age music for three minutes.

You feel wonderful, peaceful, and happy. You are ready to return.

Thank your guide.

One: You are ready to return.
Two: You feel rested.
Three: You feel wonderful in every way.
Four: You have peace of mind.
Five: You are waking up.
Six: You are ready to come back.
Seven: You are wide awake. Open your eyes.

End Notes

1. Slater Brown, *The Heyday of Spiritualism,* Mass Market Paperback, 1972, page 18.
2. http://en.wikipedia.org/wiki/Mediumship.
3. www.euro-tongil.org/swedish/english/er101.htm.
4. http://en.wikipedia.org/wiki/Eileen_J._Garrett.

Suggested Reading

Elwood Babbitt. *Talks With Christ*
Henry Leo Bolduc. *The Journey Within, Self Hypnosis*
Arthur Hasting. *On the Tongues of Angels*
Charles Hapgood. *Voices in Spirit*
Sidney Kirkpatrick. *Edgar Cayce: An American Prophet*
Jon Klimo. *Channeling*
Gordon Michael Scallion. *Notes From the Cosmos*
Jess Stearn. *The Sleeping Prophet*

Suggested Music

Krishna Das. "Flow of Grace"
Steve Halpern. "Inner Peace"
Paul Horn. "Inside the Great Pyramid"
Marcy Hamm. "Inward Harmony"
Music for Deep Meditation. "Tibetan Singing Bowls"
Carlos Nakai. "Mystic Dreamer"
Valley of the Sun. "Eternal Om"

Seventeen

What Really Happens in a Séance

If we ask a discarnate to manifest on earth for even a moment, he has to have an instrument or vehicle suitable for that, so he borrows either the mind or any of the senses that he needs of a human being... In this state of unconsciousness in which my objective mind is pushed aside there is a personality called Letcher that comes through.

~Rev. Arthur Ford

The word "séance" is French for sitting. It has come to signify a sitting in which a medium communicates with the other side of life through clairsentience, clairvoyance, clairaudience, or directly through trance. What really happens during a séance? According to Rev. Arthur Ford, a call goes out to the other side:

"We have our own version of the telephone," Fletcher (spirit guide) once reported. Word gets around to the discarnates who may be interested in the sitters at a given séance that the occasion is pending. Usually attendance is governed by what F.S.H. Meyers called "the law of love and friendship, and common interest."[1]

To begin the séance, the medium enters a light state of trance. Spirit may strengthen the connection by overshadowing the medium to placing the medium in a deeper state of trance in which the medium can remember only bits and pieces of a reading. These mediums will usually tape the session. Then there are deep trance mediums who allow spirit to take over their bodies, so communication is directly from loved ones or guides on the other side.

Deep trance mediums such as Elwood Babbitt and Arthur Ford are often unaware of the mechanics of trance. For instance when Babbitt undertook channeling the Christ force for his book, *Talks with Christ*, he became drained and had to stop for awhile. Why? The high energy was too much for his physical body, so his guide, Dr. Fisher, stepped in as an intermediary.

In Arthur Ford's trance mediumship, his guide, Fletcher, stood guard. Why is this necessary? According to the discarnate, Ruth Finley, known to the world as Edward Stewart White's wife, "Joan," in the *Unobstructed Universe*:

> In trance, another personality of about the same energy
> pattern – the control – moves in as it were to keep store. Thus
> Fletcher is in a limited way, "alive" while I have the experience
> of being "dead" – free to roam for a while in the unobstructed
> universe.[2]

The Control or spirit guide is attracted to the medium by similar energy patterns. If you think about it, this makes sense. For example, could Einstein accurately impart scientific knowledge to a ballet dancer? Or for that matter, could ballet star Anna Pavlova transmit choreography to a physicist. In each case, there would be considerable frustration.

A veteran medium is not only protected by his/her guides, but is well versed on all aspects of the séance. To begin with, intention is important. Why does the sitter wish a sitting? Is it to contact a deceased loved one, or is the purpose of the sitting to obtain six good numbers for the lottery? In the first case, a wise medium will not guarantee that a particular spirit will come through (as spirit has free will), but rather explain if that spirit is present, the medium will contact them.

English mediums are particularly fond of the validation type of reading. In America, everyone wants to know their future. Common séance questions are "When am I getting married?" for women, and for men, "When will I get a promotion?" While spirit can give positive suggestions, and even predict the future, each sitter has the free will to accept or reject advice from spirit. Basically, if you are unhappy with any aspect of the reading, you can employ free will, petition to God, and even psychological guidance to change your future.

As for the six good numbers, don't waste your time or money. Gypsy mediums may promise to give you tomorrow's lottery by casting a spell or promise to attract a new lover by burning candles, however, as with most hucksters, they promise much and deliver little if any spiritual assistance.

The skill of the medium is vital to the success of the séance. Few mediums possess the skill of the late Rev. Arthur Ford who was known to give both the first and last names of the deceased as professor Walter Uphoff discovered. He had been in Ford's apartment less than ten minutes when the medium closed his eye and began a spontaneous reading for Uphoff. Ford began by stating:

> I see a white cloud over your head... it is taking the shape of a
> face – a Slavic face – either Czech or Russian. He gave me the
> name of George Gamow.[3]

The spirit also gave his manner of death – heart disease – and provided
several personal messages to Uphoff of which Arthur Ford had no previous knowledge.

Rev. Arthur Ford was just as evidential in his public séances. For instance, when Bishop Pike contacted him after his son, Jim, committed
suicide in February of 1966, Ford agreed to do a televised séance. While
Ford was in a state of trance, his guide, Fletcher, contacted the Bishop
Pike's son who explained his suicide was the result of LSD:

> He had gotten "mixed up with the thing" in California at
> college and had fallen in with the same crowd on his return to
> New York. The suicide had been the result of a bad trip.[4]

Ford, next, brought in the names of "Donald MacKinnon," Pike's
maternal grandmother, a Russian Jew, and a Louis Pitt, who was Bishop
Pike's predecessor at Columbia University.[5]

While excellent mediums such as Rev. Arthur Ford are not usually
found in the yellow pages, there are many well-trained mediums who
sat with Spiritualist churches and camps. In more recent years, secular
organization such as Forever Friends and the Windbridge Institute have
certified mediums with extensive research and testing. The best way to
find a good medium is by word of mouth. When you make an appoint-
ment, ask the medium about his/her training and fees. A higher price
does not guarantee a better reading, so buyer beware!

Not only is it important to utilize a skilled medium, but the quality
of the sitters should also be taken into consideration. When conducting
a group séance, it is important to have like-minded people who believe
in spirit communication. Even one skeptic can bring down the energy.
High-strung sitters can drain the energy and impede communication
with the spirit world. Therefore, it is imperative that the medium screen
the sitters before the séance. If someone seems negative or emotionally
disturbed, politely let the caller know that the séance is full.

With the right attitude, a veteran medium, and sincere sitters, a séance can be an informative and even uplifting event. There are three
ways to conduct a séance – one to one, a formal séance, and public
demonstration of mediumship The solo séance is often the easiest as
the medium can directly tune into the spirits who wish to communicate.
Often, the medium will hold an article to make a quick rapport with the
sitter. Next, he or she will tune into spirits of loved one and guides. Frequently, the medium will see the person's guide standing next to them
during the reading. As for loved ones, they will usually line up in back

of the medium with those who were closest making an appearance in the séance room first.

The second type – the formal séance is when everyone sits around a round table holding hands, while the medium calls out to spirit. While presented in dramatic style in reality, formal séance is usually a quiet and very private affair. Many times people wish to have a formal séance, which is basically a group sitting by invitation only. Usually eight is good number. However, you can have as few as three or as many as sixteen if there is space around the séance table. Set a time for your séance – say 8 p.m. Have the sitters arrive early, so everyone is seated at the séance table by 8 p.m.

If you are going to deliver an introductory talk, people can arrive at 7 p.m., so there is time for the talk and a ten minute break. With a formal séance, basic protocol needs to be observed.

One: Meditate for at least thirty minutes, preferably an hour. Next, prepare the séance room. Make sure it is clean and clear any clutter. Often spirit likes to have a glass of water for each sitter, incense, or fresh flowers. Disconnect the phones, and instruct sitters to turn off cell phones. Place a tape recorder next to the medium to record the séance.

Two: As the time arrives, the medium should meditate before the séance to gain rapport with spirit. It is best to do this just before the séance. Also avoid contact with sitters prior to séance as it may look like you are fishing for information.

Three: Both medium and sitters should avoid alcoholic beverage and intoxicating drugs. These substances not only lower the energy, they can also draw negative spirits.

Four: Give a short talk. Let the sitters know before hand, that spirit exists in the astral plane and that rapport and subsequent contact may take time.

Five: Have the group assemble around a table. Everyone holds hands while the medium says a simple prayer of intention: "Loving father, Divine mother we ask for the highest good for all present. We call now on loved ones, guides, and angels to be present." After the prayer, hands can be placed in a comfortable position. Now turn on the tape recorder.

Six: Maintain silence. Wait a few minutes to gain impression. Soft music can be played. Try to maintain a positive attitude throughout the séance and a sense of humor. Mediums like Suzanne Northrop keep a light touch referring to the spirits as DPs – short for dead people. Often, mediums like the group to sing to raise the vibrations. Use songs that are easy to sing and lively such as "Jingle Bells," "I've Been Working on the Railroad" and "You Are My Sunshine."

Seven: Tune into spirit. Take your time in making contact with spirit. Have faith that spirits are there, drawn in by sincerity and devotion to a loved one. Let the sitters know beforehand, that spirit contact takes time. As Larry Dweller, author of *The Beginners Guide to Mediumship* notes:

> Remember two very important things: the spirits of the departed are everywhere in the parallel dimension (astral plane and higher planes) and the only reality spirits have in our own dimension is what we give them. By the intensity of our vibration level for reception, our intense faith we draw them near to us.[6]

Eight: When you feel spirit contact, speak directly to spirit: "Thank you for coming. Do you have a message for one of the sitters?"

Nine: Give messages as you receive them. Try to accurately place messages and give them as you receive them.

Ten: When you sense a drop in energy, let the sitters know by allowing "one last question."

Eleven: Close with a prayer of gratitude such as "We give thanks."

Twelve: Allow a few minutes for the medium to return from the world of spirit. Then turn off the tape recorder.

There is no set time for a séance. A formal séance may last from twenty minutes to an hour depending on the number of sitters. An alternative to the formal séance is the billet séance in which participants write the names of spirit they wish to contact on a slip of paper with one question on the billet (see Chapter Ten). When the sitter signs his or her name, spirit receives the question. These billets are filled out while the medium is out of the room and collected by an assistant. The medium is securely blind-folded. Next, a prayer of intention is said such as the "Lord's Prayer." By using psychometry, the medium holds each billet and gives his or her impression. This type of séance has gone out of style for two reasons: one, the lack of skilled mediums, and two, fake mediums employing the one-up method to cheat. However, this method can be used honestly and successfully with sincere practice.

While a billet séance is by invitation only, a public séance is dependent on the organization which sponsors it, so there is less control. Even in a Spiritualist church, anyone off the street can walk in for a reading. It is important to preface your demonstration with a short talk and some rules. First, find out if it is okay to do a reading. Simply ask, "May I come to you?" If the person shakes his/her head or says "No," go on to the next person. Also let people know spirit needs their voice for rapport. Ask each person to say hello or give their first name. Just as in the formal séance, give what you receive.

There are two methods for conducting a public demonstration of mediumship. In Spiritualist churches, the medium goes to the sitter in the audience and asks, "May I come to you and give a message?" For instance, "I see a tall gray-haired man who always wore a white shirt and dark suit to work. He looks about 60 as he died just short of retirement." Then when the sitter say, "Oh, that was my Dad, Jim; he was an accountant," you have the voice connection to continue the reading.

The second method is to simply give up names and descriptions without placing them, as they do at Camp Chesterfield in Indiana. For example, a medium may say, "I have Jim here who died at about 60. Two people may call out, "I know a Jim in spirit." The Medium may then say, "He always wore a white shirt and dark suit to work." Then one person may say, "That was my Dad who was a banker." When doing group readings, familiarize yourself with the method preferred and rules that the organization may have. For example, in English Spiritualist churches, they focus on validation readings, and are not partial to descriptions of guides or even the future which cannot be validated at the moment of the reading. Spiritualist churches, such as those belonging to the National Association of Spiritualist Churches in the United States, will not allow any mention of reincarnation on the platform, while independent camps such Camp Cassadaga in Florida and the Spiritualist Alliance does allow for statements about reincarnation.

Finally, when working with the public, a medium has to be prepared for skeptics. Sometimes evangelical Christians will attend a public séance only to stir up trouble. The best way to handle their negativity is by saying, "I will be happy to talk to you after the service," and quickly go on to the next person. At the end of the service, take a few minutes to politely answer their concerns. Often, the devout Christian wants to know if the spirits are evil. Talk to the concerned sitter in a polite manner. Explain spiritual service such as mediumship is based on vibration. Like attracts like. Since you have meditated before the service for only the highest and best for all present, you feel assured the spirits come in to serve humanity If the person wishes more information, refer him or her the literature listed at the end of the chapter.

Give careful thought before agreeing to do a public séance. What are the group's motives? Ask your guides for advice before accepting. If you accept, allow for less than ideal conditions. However, remember like attracts like. If you are sincere in your desire to share spirit, you are likely to attract an enthusiastic audience.

Suggestions for Public Demonstration of Mediumship

Meditate before your demonstration. Call on your guides to be present.

Introduce yourself in a pleasant but clear voice. Give your credentials. For example: "My name is Elaine Kuzmeskus, I am a certified Spiritualist medium, and author of *Connecticut Ghosts* and *Séance 101*.

Tune into spirit. Focus carefully on these areas:

- Male or female
- Relation to sitter
- Approximate age
- Body build
- Hair color, eye color, other facial features such as a beard or glasses
- Clothing
- Manner of death
- Describe where they lived-- either home or location of home
- Profession
- Hobbies
- Family ties
- A name or initial, if possible
- Sometimes spirit will call out the name of their loved one
- Any pertinent details spirit wishes to present
- A brief message

Use all your psychic skills – intuition, clairaudience, or clairvoyance. Once you connect with spirit, locate the right sitter. Next, ask permission with a brief remark such as: "May I come to you?" or "Spirit has a message for you." If the sitter agrees (and he/she usually does), then ask "May I have your first name please?" The sound of the person's voice is needed to increase rapport with spirit.

Then give a brief description of spirit. Include physical appearance, relationship to sitter, occupation, manner of death, hobbies, and a message.

Keep a sense of humor and be diplomatic. For example, if you sense the spirit had a drinking problem, you might say, "Uncle Peter liked his beer." Also avoid diagnosing illness as this is against the law. Avoid skeptics. Use tactics such as, " I will be happy to discuss this with you after the service," and quickly turn to the next person.

Elaine M. Kuzmeskus at Lily Dale Assembly, New York delivering a lecture.

End Notes

1. Arthur Ford, *Unknown but Known,* Harper and Row, New York, NY, 1968, page 66.
2. Arthur Ford, *Unknown but Known,* Harper and Row, New York, NY, 1968, page 67-68.
3. Walter and Mary Jo Uphoff, *New Psychic Frontiers,* Colin Symnthe Limited, Gerrards Cross, ngland, (1980) page 57.
4. Arthur Ford, *Unknown but Known,* Harper and Row, New York, NY, 1968, page 72.
5. Arthur Ford, *Unknown but Known,* Harper and Row, New York, NY, 1968, page 73.
6. Larry Dweller, *Beginner's Guide to Mediumship,* page 57.

Suggested Reading

Raymond Buckland. *The Book of Spirits*
Larry Dweller. *Beginner's Guide to Mediumship*
Suzanne R. Giesemann. *The Medium and the Priest*
Arthur Ford. *Unknown but Known*
Ivy Northage. *Mediumship Made Simple*
Suzanne Northrop. *Séance*

Eighteen

A Professional Medium

A shimmer and shake do not a medium make.

~Spiritualist proverb

Mediumship is an emerging, but very important field, of human potential. As a professional medium, I have done it all – private sittings, group readings, college lectures with demonstrations to large audiences, as well as stage séances before standing-room-only crowds. Sometimes, it takes nerves of steel, and other times, complete relaxation. At every event, whether the audience is warm or wary, I feel confident, that spirit is present Why? My training. For three years, I sat in a circle with Rev. Kenneth and Gladys Custance, spent Sundays serving the First Spiritualist Church of Onset, and was tested by other mediums to prove my ability to communicate with spirit. When I received my mediumship certificate, I was ready to work with the public.

It is only natural to have some doubts as you begin your medium-ship, but remember, you are in control. As you relax and tune in with intuition, clairvoyance, and clairaudience, your guides can direct you. Recently, a friend, Denise, called very distraught. "Can you help me, Elaine?" she said. "We are afraid he has stopped taking his medication for bipolar and is in a manic state." (Apparently, his parents had not heard from their twenty-four year-old son for several days.) When they flew out to California, his apartment was vacant, which made them fear the worst – perhaps Jeremy was never coming home. After expressing my sympathy, I took a deep breath and immediately saw a picture of Jeremy dazed and driving aimlessly around in his car. Then within seconds, I heard the sounds of a police car behind him. I "knew" that Jeremy was alive and most probably would be picked up by the police. By the end of the day, Denise called back to tell me her nephew was spotted by a cruiser and was brought into the station.

Of course, not all stories have a happy ending. Sometimes a medium is called upon to do psychic detective work. That same day, a client, a

146

police officer, came with a photo of an attractive waif-like blonde young woman, Katy. When I looked at the photo, I said: "She died suddenly, her life was taken from her." Then I felt an extreme rush of anger – and added: "She knew her murderer." After that, all I could do was confirm the gruesome details of the murder by Katy's on and off again boyfriend. "I told her so many times not to go back with him," said the broad shouldered detective, wiping a tear from his eyes.

A medium may also encounter non-believers. When I was at a local Barnes and Noble bookstore to do a book signing for my biography, *The Making of a Medium,* I was disappointed to see only four people in attendance, so I suggested to the public relations director, "Why don't you announce over the loud speaker, "'The author will be doing psychic readings.'" Within minutes, we had a crowd of believers and non- believers. As I was giving readings, I was impressed to go to a college student. I gave her a message from her mother's grandmother, Helen. After "Helen" spoke, the young lady just shrugged, "I don't even know the name of my mother's grandmother." Her great grandmother must have been stubborn because I heard myself saying, "Why don't you just call your mother and find out?" Ten minutes later, the skeptical young woman came back. "I just called my mother and her grandmother's name was Helen!" Spirit had made a believer out of her great-granddaughter.

As you can see from these examples, mediumship is a serious business. That is why I started the New England School of Metaphysics in 1997, to help people become professional mediums, healers, and astrologers. At the New England School of Metaphysics, students take twenty-four-week "Basics of Mediumship" courses and then go on to specialize in mental mediumship, trance mediumship, or healing. Of course, all of this training takes time. Usually, it takes three to five years to fully unfold mediumship.

As the old-time Spiritualists warn: "A shimmer and shake do not a medium make." Mediumship needs to be demonstrated on a regular basis – not just a shimmer every now and then. Spiritualists such as Kenneth and Gladys Custance insisted on consistent validation messages. For example, Mrs. Custance would ask students to describe the spirit, tell the manner of death, and possibly give a name or initial. Only then would she encourage her students to give a message from spirit. It is just too easy to say: "I have an older lady, your grandmother, she brings in love." While that may be true, it is not validation. However, if a medium described a tall woman with short white hair, who loved to play cards, and always wore pearls, the sitter will know that grandmother is indeed there. Then the message, "Your grandmother bring love," has real meaning.

Rev. Arthur Ford, a friend of the Custances, was one the best mediums. As mentioned, he was known to give both the first and last names of the deceased. Ford became well known in January 7 1929, when he brought through several evidential messages from the magician to his wife, Bess Houdini, which Houdini's widow validated. Later he conducted séances for Rev. Sun Myung Moon who was amazed by the medium's ability to bring through first and last names of the deceased:

> In a sitting on November 1964, Ford said Fletcher mentioned Pieter Alexander, who had learned about Sun Myung Moon's ideas on spiritual growth.[1]

Later, Arthur Ford conducted the first televised network séance when he made contact with the dead son of Bishop Pike in 1967.

While a public séance often puts the medium on the spot, in a private sitting, the medium has more time to connect with spirit and to bring comfort to the bereaved. This is important as those who have recently lost a loved one can be very vulnerable. Not only do they need reassurance that the loved one has survived, they need assistance with their intense grief. People frequently ask me how long they should wait before I make contact with spirit? Often our loved ones come through in the first critical hours after death. In fact, I often see the spirit of the deceased standing right next to relatives as mourners pass by the coffin.

Just as it takes the living time to accept the loss, it also takes spirit time to adjust to death. If you visit a medium too soon, the spirit of your loved one may not have sufficient energy to manifest. That is why I usually suggest waiting a month before consulting a medium. Sometimes if the mourner comes too soon, their loved one does not have the strength to come through. When a deceased relative does come though, the spirit will relay messages such as "I knew I was dead because I no longer was in pain," or "I saw my mother and father who greeted me."

Many times, spirit is more at peace than those they left behind. Sometimes the hardest part of grieving is learning what to do with all the love they shared. As the medium, I can reassure them love does not end at the grave. "Please know that your loved one is only a thought away," I tell those who are deep in grief. Spirit is disturbed by prolonged grief and it makes the link between the two worlds weaker. When your deceased loved one comes to mind, send a loving thought out and know it is received on the other side. If I feel the sitter needs more than validation to deal with grief, I recommend professional counseling. Psychologists today are well equipped through the work of the late Dr. Elisabeth Kubler-Ross to assist patient through the stages of death and dying.

James Van Praagh has written an excellent book on the subject, *Healing Grief: Reclaiming Life After Loss*. When I first began to visit Lily Dale Assembly, I attended one of Van Praagh's seminars. I had been a fan of his program, "The Other Side," and his bestselling book, *Talking to Heaven*. I wasn't disappointed as James Van Praagh's humor and showmanship made for a lively demonstration of spirit communication.

The highlight of the seminar was his healing meditation, during which I "saw" the many spirit doctors and nurses who assisted the medium.

Of course, it is not unusual to contact spirit at Lily Dale. For instance, when Ron and I stayed in Assembly Hall, where guest mediums are housed, my husband woke up to spirit voices. In a jovial mood, he had picked up an antique copper trumpet and placed it at the foot of our bed, just as we were retiring for the evening. "Maybe it will float during the night," he said. I just laughed at the thought. Sure enough, that evening in Room Two, the trumpet was active. Ron was awakened in the middle of the night by the sound of the trumpet moving and voices streaming forth!

While I find spiritual phenomena fascinating, I am more focused on research. Lily Dale has one of the finest libraries on mediumship in the country. I have spent countless hours reviewing volumes at the Skidmore Library, as well as the smaller library at the National Association of Spiritualist Churches headquarter, reading about the pioneers of Spiritualism.

Another favorite spot is the Lily Dale Museum. Curator Ron Nagy has been most helpful in locating the names of trumpet mediums and pointing out details in the many precipitated paintings housed in the Museum. According to Ron:

> No one knows exactly how, or under what circumstances, precipitated spirit paintings started, but as in most instances, the first phenomena occurred with the mediums unaware of what was happening or why. The first recorded demonstration of precipitated spirit painting was in the year 1894 by the Bangs Sisters.[3]

Nagy is also an author of two books on mediumship: *Precipitated Paintings* and *Slate Writing: Invisible Intelligences.*

Another Spiritualist center filled with fascinating artifacts is the Arthur Findlay College in London. In 2002, Ron and I took a trip to England to attend the Arthur Findlay College just outside of London. The college is Findlay's elegant estate which he donated to the Spiritualists. The stately mansion is filled with antiques, oriental rugs, and portraits of ancestors, as well as many fine spirit photographs. The spiritual college is very proper and quintessential British. It even has a pub in the basement! I was a little nervous Ron might not take his trance mediumship class seriously. However, he quickly joined in and made many friends.

While I enjoyed the English mediums, I was surprised how much emphasis was placed on identifying spirit. Basically, the English mediums do validation readings, taking great care to describe features and personality of the deceased, manner of death, and, occupation. In the United States, we also emphasize the identification of guides and prophecy. We constantly heard groans of, "You Americans," as the British shook their heads at our far-fetched ideas.

After the week-long seminar, we toured London with our friends Stanley and Mary Ellen. We all loved the double-decker buses, but had our share of difficulty on the "tube." The British warned us in a printed sign there would be a sound and then the tube doors would shut. We had no idea what this meant. Poor Mary Ellen was left behind when door shut as she struggled to get her luggage out. "Get off at the next stop," I yelled to a very nervous Mary Ellen. About an hour later we managed to retrieve her at the next station. Of course, the bobbies had a good laugh when we told them our plight. Once we arrived in London, we enjoyed three wonderful days filled with strolls through Hyde Park, shopping trips to Bond Street, and meals at the local pub, the Black Swan.

For those interested in physical phenomena, Camp Chesterfield in Indiana offers trumpet séances and a superior museum filled with precipitated paintings of the Bangs Sisters as well as other spirit artists. The camp is about a ten-hour car ride from Connecticut which makes for a good road trip. In April 2005, I visited Camp Chesterfield to take a class: "Introduction to the Séance Room" with Rev. Suzanne Greer. I was most interested in attending as the class ended with a trumpet séance. Rev. Greer, who is of Hungarian ancestry, is passionate about mediumship. She suggested that we all read *101 Questions and Answers* by Peggy Barnes. Having been at the camp for over thirty years, Susie had many stories of Camp Chesterfield's physical mediums, such as Pansy Cox who materialized spirit and past camp President Mamie Schultz Brown, also known for her physical mediumship. Rev. Greer was a stickler for accurate messages. She was quick to correct a student who excused a message with, "Well, spirit told me." "Remember," she reminded her pupil, "You are in control of spirit."

The highlight of the class is the last session in which Rev. Suzanne Greer, who sat for fifteen years to become a trumpet medium, conducts a trumpet séance. By the time the class assembled, we had all been well-prepared for the séance both physically and mentally. The séance was conducted in the completely black basement séance room. The medium took her place in a spirit cabinet to prepare herself for the dead trance necessary to conduct the trumpet séance. Meanwhile, the students asked to sing several songs to lift the vibration. As we sang songs, such as "Jingle Bells," a favorite of the spirit guide, Penny, the energy in the room seemed thick with ectoplasm. Within minutes of being seated, I was fortunate to witness the trumpet lift and act as a megaphone to the spirit world. Everyone present could hear the voices of their loved ones. Suzanne even lowered the trumpet, so we could all feel it tap us on our toes!

There are several other trumpet mediums at Camp Chesterfield. Rev. Louise Irvine gave a wonderful two-hour demonstration of an Ascended Master trumpet séance in which the Ascended Masters spoke. While the philosophy was wonderful, no personal messages were given. Another highlight of my first trip to Camp Chesterfield was taking a meditation class with Rev. Patricia Kennedy in the Hett Auditorium. Pat Kennedy had many fine pointers on the art of meditation as well as her amazing life. We just loved the energy of the auditorium which is filled with precipitated paintings of the Bangs Sisters. One observer, Mr. Moore, descried the phenomena:

> After a quarter of an hour, the outlines of shadows began to appear and disappear as if the invisible artist was making a preliminary sketch, then the picture began to grow at a feverish rate. When the frames were separated the portrait was found on the paper surface of the canvas next to the sitter. Although the paint was greasy and stuck to the finger on being touched, it left no stain on the paper surface of the other canvas, which closely covered it.[4]

Amazingly, the portraits of deceased relatives and friends still retain their vibrant colors more than a hundred years later. If for no other reason, the precipitated paintings are worth a trip to Camp Chesterfield.

In 2007, we made a trip to Brazil. Ron was having problems with knees which he had injured while playing; we hoped that he would receive a healing. When we returned from England, we sought out healing services from John of God first in Atlanta, Georgia. We both were blessed to have "invisible procedures" which left us in an intense state of healing for about twenty-four hours. In fact , Ron had two such procedures with good results. When he returned home, he discovered that a tumor about the size of a gold ball in his left arm had disappeared!

While we were in Atlanta, John of God, said to Ron, "Come to Brazil," so we decided to go to Brazil for more healing. Our friend, Mary Arendt, accompanied us on our adventure. Since the trip had several delays, including a unexpected stay in San Paulo, we were especially happy to see Heather Cumming, our tour guide at the airport in Brasilia. Heather, the consummate hostess, guided us on a tour of the city and its many fine churches. We also had our first Brazilian barbecue. As a vegetarian, I enjoyed the salad bar and the white chocolate cake, while Ron devoured his fair share of beef, pork, and chicken. When we arrived, we were given cards to let the waiter know how much meat the patron wished. When Ron had had enough meat, he turned his card over to let the waiter know he was full.

Of course, the best part of our trip was meeting with John of God. While in trance, spirit doctors, such as Doctor Cruz, came through for advice. When it came my turn to talk to the entity, I brought a copy of *Séance 101* and asked for a blessing. When the spirit guide heard that John of God was in the book, he accepted it and asked for three more copies. I was so pleased. The reason for the trip was the invisible surgeries which were immensely powerful. Fortunately, we had them on separate days, so we could help each other as we all needed to rest in our rooms for a day. The energy in the room was incredible. The spirit guides or "entities" do the invisible surgery with precision. I felt no pain, just "buzzed out." Soon, I felt uplifted and about ten years younger. When I returned to the states, friends said, "You have never looked better." I felt great. Not only had I shed ten pounds, but my blood work also indicated optimum health as well.

Finally, in January 2010, I made my first trip to the Spiritualist camp founded by George Colby. As Ron and I pulled into the hotel parking lot of Camp Cassadaga, I was dismayed to see neon signs announcing Tarot readings from across the street. "You know, Ron," I said, "mediums are not supposed to use Tarot cards – only their psychic skills." With some misgivings, we checked into Hotel Cassadaga, a white Art Deco structure built in 1927. However, we felt reassured when we visited the bookstore/information center where we found the spirit of Spiritualism very evident in the many books on mediumship and psychic phenomena.

In its heyday in the 1920s, Cassadaga attracted stellar mediums such as the famous physical medium, Mabel Riffle, whose Sunday evening séances brought the largest audience ever recorded at Cassadaga. No wonder.

> Typically for forty minutes at a time, the great message bearer would roll out "name after name, fact after fact, in an endless stream that delighted the audience, confounded the critics, and filled investigators with wonder."[5]

As Cassadaga grew in popularity, even the wife of Florida senator Duncan Fletcher defeated Spiritualism before a House subcommittee, and later, in 1926, published a book on the subject entitled *Death Unveiled.*[6] With such a rich history, Ron and I were excited at the prospect of attending the Saturday night orb tour. The highlight of the tour was a visit to Colby Temple that houses a séance room which the old-time mediums used for physical phenomena. While only physical mediums were allowed in the room, tourists were allowed to take photographs from the door way. Shivers went up my spine as we peered in. Apparently, Ron and I were not alone as seen in this series of photographs showing an eight-foot column of white ectoplasm in the center of the séance room. The column literally is moving across the room as you can see from the series of photographs at the end of the chapter.

While the spirit world intertwines with our own, only a few are able to capture its image on film or for that matter tune into its reality.

Vortex pictures taken in sequence
in a church seance room.
Photographer: Ronald Kuzmeskus

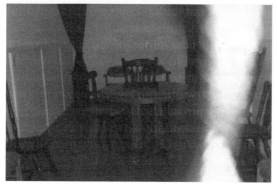

A Final Word

Whatever your interest in mediumship – spirit photography, ghost hunting, psychic detective work, medical clairvoyance, or séances, I do hope the book has given you a better understanding of how the spirit world intertwines with our own. Meanwhile, for those students who are ready for professional mediumship, the teacher will appear.

~Elaine Kusmeskus

Resources

Cassadaga Spiritualist Camp
1325 Stevens Street
P.O. Box 319
Cassadaga, FL 32706

Camp Chesterfield
P.O. Box 132
50 Lincoln Drive
Chesterfield, IN 46017

Arthur Findlay College
Standsted Hall,
Stansted Mountfitchet,
Essex, United Kingdom
CM 24 8UD

Forever Family Foundation, Inc.
222 Atlantic Avenue
Oceanside, NY 11572

Lily Dale Assembly
5 Melrose Park
P.O. Box 248
Lily Dale, NY 14752

New England School of Metaphysics
1316 Spruce Street
Suffield, CT 06078

Windbridge Institute, LLC
1517 N. Wilmot Rd. #254
Tucson, AZ 85712

End Notes

1. http://en.wikipedia.org/wiki/Arthur_Ford.
2. Reverend John Sullivan, Spiritualist medium.
3. www.ronnagy.net.
4. www.Answers.com/topic/bangs-sisters.
5. John Gunthrie Jr., Phillip Charles De Lucas, Gary Monroe, Cassadaga, the South'sOldest Spiritualist Camp, University of Florida Press, Gainesville, FL, 2000, page 47.
6. John Gunthrie Jr., Phillip Charles De Lucas, Gary Monroe, Cassadaga, the South's Oldest Spiritualist Camp, University of Florida Press, Gainesville, FL, 2000, page 48.

Glossary

Apport: A gift materialized by spirit at a séance. Usually a small article such as a stone, a ring, or even a feather.

Billet: A note to spirit written on a small piece of paper.

Cabinet: A closet, curtained off corner of a room, or a wooden spirit cabinet used in physical mediumship.

Chakra: Energy circles in the etheric body.

Channeling: The ability to contact spirit directly through trance mediumship. This is a modern term for full-trance mediumship.

Clairaudience: The ability to hear spirit voices and spirit music. Often the sound seems to come from a distance. This is because spirit may form an astral tube to amplify the sound.

Clairgustance: The ability to smell scents from the other side, such perfume, cigars, or apple pie. Sometimes this term is used to refer to the taste of spirit, such as the taste of apple pie.

Clairsentience: The ability to sense or intuit the presence of spirit. The medium feels or senses the presence of spirit. Sometimes this is accompanied by a change in temperature, literally the air on the medium's arms raise, or he/she may feel a chill down the back.

Clairvoyance: The ability to see spirit though the third or psychic eye. Often this gift begins with seeing pinpoint lights and colors. A medium may see spirit or objectively in front of him/her or subjectively in the mind's eye.

Direct Voice: Spirit voices that can be heard by everyone in the séance room.

Ectoplasm: A white substance that is extruded from the body of the medium for the purposes of materialization.

Electromagnetic Field Meter: The EMF meter is a gauge used by ghost hunters to detect changes in the electromagnetic fields which can indicate spirit activity.

Electronic Voice Phenomena: EVP is the ability to record spirit sounds or even voices on a tape recorder.

K2 Meter: A devise used to detect magnetic fields.

Guide: A deceased person, such as a relative, or religious figure who helps the living. Some guides, such as angels, have never incarnated.

Levitation: The ability to move objects. Sometimes referred to as psychokinesis. It also refers to the ability of mediums, such as D.D. Home, floating above the ground.

Materialization: Appearance of spirit through formation of ectoplasm from a medium. This may be either full-figure or a partial materialization of a face or hand during a séance.

Medium: A sensitive person who acts as an agent between this earth and the other side.

Mental Mediumship: The ability to contact the other side through clairsentience, clairaudience, clairvoyance, or clairgustance.

Natural Law: Principles of nature which includes the human, animal, vegetable, and mineral kingdoms.

Physical Medium: The ability to contact the other side through physical phenomena such as table tipping, electronic voice phenomena, psychic photography, direct voice, materialization, and apports.

Precipitated Paintings/Pictures: These are pictures which have been formed or precipitated by spirit artists.

Possession The rare phenomena of a spirit entity taking over the body of a living person without the person's permission.

Psychic Photography: The act of capturing the image of spirit in a photograph. Sometimes referred to as spirit photography. Many times, these images do not show up until the picture is developed.

Psychokinesis (PK): Movement of objects and people without any physical means of support.

Psychometry: The ability to read energy by holding an object, such as a watch or a ring. A medium can pick up vibrations of the past, present and future for the owner.

Skotograph: Spirit photograph usually done in the dark without the use of a camera.

Slate Writing: The practice of spirit writing messages on slates.

Spiritualism: The religion, science, and philosophy based on the belief in: "There is no death and there are no dead."

Table Tipping: Communicating with spirit via spirit raps from within the table.

Third Eye: The sixth psychic center located in the middle of the forehead which is associated with psychic vision.

Trance: An altered state of consciousness which can range from light trance (Alpha level) to medium trance (Theta level) to dead trance (Delta level).

Transfiguration: A mask of ectoplasm covering the medium's features so that the face of Spirit appears.

Trumpet: A light-weight cone used for physical mediumship. It usually is made of aluminum or copper.

Index